POCKET GUIDE
to
IRISH
GENEALOGY

Second Edition

POCKET GUIDE
to
I R I S H
GENEALOGY

Second Edition

Brian Mitchell

CLEARFIELD

Printed for
Clearfield Company, Inc. by
Genealogical Publishing Co., Inc.
Baltimore, Maryland
2002

International Standard Book Number: 0-8063-5122-5
Made in the United States of America

CONTENTS

GENEALOGY - AN ENJOYABLE HOBBY

"If you understand a man the first time you meet him, there isn't much in him to understand. And you won't understand Robert McCook at the start, for he is an Irishman, and a deep one at that. A big lump of a man--6 feet 2 inches in his socks--broad, thick-chested, going bald on top. You'd pick him out as a farmer if you met him on board ship or in a cafe in Paris. He looks the part." This is how the *Dairy Bulletin* of June 1910 described Robert McCook, then the owner of a big herd of Jersey milking cows in Brisbane, Australia, but formerly a farmer's son from Garvagh, Co. Londonderry. With this information I began my research into the McCook families of Ireland, Australia and New Zealand, and what a story it turned out to be.

Two Sunday afternoon chats around the fireside with 87-year-old Robert Graham, who now owns the McCook farm in Garvagh, enabled me to virtually tie up the McCook family tree in Ireland for descendants of McCooks living in New Zealand and Australia. Robert, leaning slightly forward on his walking stick, his eyes bright with recollection, recalled for a total of six hours the McCook family history.

The identification of a McCook gravestone in the graveyard attached to the old first Garvagh Presbyterian Church (now demolished) and a search of the baptism registers of that church and of the 1901 census returns for the Garvagh area allowed me to complete the McCook story. It began around 1860 when Alexander McCook bought a farm at Edenbane, near Garvagh. He married and raised a large family, with the six eldest sons, Archibald, Alexander, Graham, William, James, and John, emigrating to Queensland, Australia. From John were descended the "Fighting McCooks" of New Zealand. John had arrived in Brisbane in January 1866, and from there he turned to farming in Auckland, New Zealand. He had 12 children, including four boys, Peter, John, William, and James, who all served in the New Zealand forces in World War One and were either wounded or gassed, three in France and one at Gallipoli in 1915.

Alexander's youngest son Robert, the subject of the article in the *Dairy Bulletin*, at first stayed behind to farm the family farm at Edenbane, but on the death of his mother Jane in 1881 he sold the family farm and in 1883 followed his six elder brothers to Queensland. There were now no male descendants of Alexander McCook in the Garvagh area, but in the 1890s Archibald, the eldest son, returned and bought a farm at the Grove, Moyletra Toy, an adjoining townland to Edenbane. He married and Archibald's 13 children were baptized at First Garvagh Presbyterian Church. In the early 1900s five of Archibald's sons, Alexander, James, William, John and Robert emigrated to the gold mines of Kalgoorlie in Western Australia. The youngest son Hugh remained and farmed at the Grove. Hugh married Robert Graham's sister, but they had no children. With Hugh's death, on 24 April 1960, the McCook surname died out in the Garvagh area. The McCook farmstead still stands, a solid two-storey house, which at one time was home to 13 children. It now lies empty and derelict, only Robert Graham's cattle being in evidence, and adjoining the house is a substantial walled garden with tree stumps inside of a one-time orchard. In its day this was obviously a fertile farm. By contrast the McCooks in New Zealand and Australia are flourishing.

This one example sums up for me what makes genealogy and the study of one's family tree such an absorbing and fascinating pastime. The attraction for me lies in building up a picture--piece by piece--of your ancestry utilizing people's memories and historical records. The detective work in building up a family tree is just as rewarding as the identification of a family line.

The basic aim of this book is to overcome the perception that genealogy is only for the experts. The piecing together of one's family tree is not only enjoyable but relatively straightforward. I have found through twenty years' involvement in genealogy as a tutor and manager of a genealogy centre that the examination of only seven major records will throw quite detailed light on most peoples' Irish ancestry. The records being civil registers, parish registers, gravestone inscriptions, wills, the 1901 or 1911 census, Griffith's Valuation and Tithe Applotment Books. With these records most people should be able to build up a family tree going back six or seven generations on most family lines. This is a substantial number of ancestors and an equally substantial number of interesting family stories, as by the seventh generation every individual will be directly descended from 64 great great great great grandparents. I intend to show how to initiate a family tree search in Ireland, and how to make the best use of the seven major record sources to fill in family detail.

There are obviously more than seven records in Ireland which are genealogically useful, and many of them are briefly described in this book. This doesn't affect my basic premise that for most people the research of seven major records is all that is required to build up a detailed family tree. Glossaries are included at the back of the book explaining the major administrative divisions and listing the major record offices and heritage centres in Ireland. Against each record office is given its address and telephone number, opening hours, record sources held and any observations that might be of interest to a researcher. Refer to the glossaries as often as required when reading the book.

This book will be of interest to those people of Irish descent living outside Ireland, as a section is included to show briefly what they should do in their home country before tracing the family's roots in Ireland.

IRISH HISTORY AND GENEALOGY

Between the fourth and seventh centuries A.D., Ireland underwent a series of large-scale changes which saw the emergence of new ruling dynasties, as the earlier peoples were pushed into the background, and the penetration of Christianity into the country. The ancient genealogists then got to work to confirm the new status quo and endowed the rising dynasties with ancestors whose names included the first element of their names. The ruling clans boasted descent from the founder of the dynasty as the prestige of a King was derived from a pedigree of kings with origin-legends in pagan times.

By 700 A.D., the north of the country was dominated by the Connachta, i.e. descendants of Conn, and by their most important branch the Ui Neill, i.e. descendants of Niall, who were descended according to genealogical lore from "Conn of the Hundred Battles." Whether Conn was a god, an idol or a real person is immaterial. What is certain, however, is that his "descendants" pushed eastwards and northwards out of Connaught, capturing Tara and taking sword land as far north as Inishowen, County Donegal. This expansion was assigned by the genealogists to "Niall of the Nine Hostages," King of Tara in the early 400s, and his fourteen sons. The by-product of this northward expansion was the pushing out of the existing peoples of the Kingdom of Dal Riada in Ulster across the Irish channel to Argyll, Scotland and the founding of the Kingdom of Scots about 490 A.D.

The southern half of Ireland was dominated by the royal families of the Eoganachta, i.e. descendants of Eogan, from their base at Cashel. Eogan, meaning "born of the yew tree," was in all probability the name of a pagan god spirit, although it is possible that Eogan was a real king living around 300 A.D. It is historical fact, however, that by the second half of the sixth century the Eoganachta were over-kings of Munster.

The end result of this emergence of new dynasties is that the major Irish families have reliable genealogies dating from 550 A.D., as historical fact begins to take over from origin-legend. Today the descendants of these Irish dynastic families are the oldest authenticated male-line families surviving in Europe.

By the second half of the sixth century, the outlines of later political geography were becoming visible. The tuath, or kingdom, was the basic political unit. There were 90 such kingdoms in Ireland. As kingship was in the possession of an extended kin-group, known as the derbfine, in which all those males with a great grandfather in common were eligible for kingship, each and every branch of the family tree of the dynastic kingship group had to be accounted for. In Gaelic society the poets or Filidh were the custodians of the history and genealogy of the clans. This body of genealogical material is scattered throughout early literature and is preserved in a series of manuscripts, written from the twelfth century in a mixture of Latin and Gaelic. In these pedigrees will be found the names of thousands of people, many of whom will not be recorded in any other historical source.

To the eleventh century the different families of the clan were held together by the tradition of common descent from an ancestor who had lived many centuries ago. From the eleventh century each family began to adopt its own distinctive family name, generally derived from an ancestor who lived in or about the tenth century. The old political unit, the tuath, now became subdivided into family clans or septs. The term sept means a group of persons who or whose immediate ancestors bore a common name and inhabited the same locality.

Irish surnames were formed by prefixing either "Mac" to the father's name, meaning "son of," or "O" to that of a grandfather or earlier ancestor, meaning "descendant of." The O'Neills of Ulster took their name from Nial Glundubh, High King of Ireland who was killed in 919 besieging the Danes in Dublin. Brian Boru, High King of Ireland killed by the Danes at Clontarf in 1014, was the ancestor of the O'Briens of Munster, while the O'Connors of Connaught were descended from Chonchobar, King of Connaught, who died in 971. Irish surnames, therefore, can be equated with their own unique history and geography.

In the twelfth century a new set of surnames, belonging to the families of the Norman invaders, was introduced to Ireland. The Normans were eventually assimilated and their names such as Burke, Costello, Cusack, Dalton, Dillon, Fitzgerald, Nugent, Power, Roche and Walsh became regarded as Irish as the great Gaelic names of O'Neill, O'Connor and O'Brien.

A new dimension to the Irish landscape, and of extreme genealogical significance, was added from the 17th century. The defeat of the Ulster rebellion led by Hugh O'Neill in 1603 and the flight of the chiefs of Ulster to the Continent in 1607 offered an opportunity for the re-settlement of large parts of Ulster on an entirely new basis. Land in the six counties of Armagh, Cavan, Coleraine (renamed Londonderry), Donegal, Fermanagh and Tyrone had been forfeited. In 1609 the Earl of Salisbury suggested to James I a deliberate plantation of English and Scottish colonists. Unlike the plantation of the Americas which was going on at this time, where colonisation was to further the economic interest of the mother country, that in Ulster was primarily strategic. It was felt that the only way to prevent another rebellion in Ulster was to create a plantation strong enough to resist the native Irish. The size of the estate, the number of tenants, the type of settlement, as well as religion, education and defence were all provided for in the plan. The first wave of settlers came to Ulster as lessees of the numerous proprietors who were granted estates by James I in the period 1605 to 1625. The second wave came after 1652 with Cromwell's crushing of the Irish rebellion, when eleven million acres of land were confiscated. This Cromwellian settlement led to a flood of new English settlers. By 1672 Sir William Petty estimated that the population of Ireland consisted of 800,000 Irish, 200,000 English and 100,000 Scots. The third and final wave of immigrants came after the Glorious Revolution. In the ten or fifteen years after 1690 it is estimated that 50,000 people came to Ulster from Scotland. By 1703 85% of all the land of Ireland had been confiscated from Catholic ownership and transferred to Protestant possession. By 1715 the Presbyterian population of Ulster, i.e. of essentially Scottish origin, stood at 200,000.

Unlike the Norman settlement there was little assimilation between the new settlers and the old inhabitants. The most striking feature of the English and Scottish surnames introduced into Ireland and especially Ulster was their great number and variety. In 1856 of the 50 most common surnames in England, 27 were derived from Christian names, 13 from occupations, seven from localities, two from personal characteristics, namely Brown and White, and one other, namely King. Welsh names were often formed from the Christian name of the father in the genitive case, thus John's son became Jones and Evan's son became Evans.

Plantation names can give clues to the origins of people holding that surname. For example, I traced the Sintons of Rockmacreeny in Kilmore Parish, County Armagh back to Crewcat in the same parish and from there to Scotland. In a will dated 20 December 1735, Jacob Sinton of Crewcat received William Mackie's farm at Rockmacreeny. Jacob had married William's daughter Sarah in Ballyhagan Quaker meeting house on 6 August 1730. This Jacob Sinton, according to tradition, was the son of Joseph Sinton who was born about 1680, the first-born son of Judge Isaac Swinton who was supposed to have come from Scotland to Moyallon, County Down around 1690.

Swinton is one of the earliest known surnames in Scotland, dating from the eleventh century, their name being derived from the land which they are said to have received in reward of their prowess in destroying herds of wild boars which then infested North Berwickshire. It is, however, more probable that the Sintons originated from Selkirkshire, also in the Borders of Scotland. I went to the town of Selkirk, and just to the south of it I found the placenames of Synton, North Synton, Synton Mossend, Synton Mains and Synton Parkhead. And there lies the clue to the origin of Sintons in Ulster. They took their name from the ancient barony of Synton, now in the parish of Ashkirk. Around the turn of the thirteenth century the Sheriffdom of Selkirk was given to one Andrew de Synton. This doesn't mean all Sintons of Scottish origin are descended from Andrew Synton, as tenants often took the name of their landlord. A search of the pre-1720 entries in the baptism registers of the area came up with five Sinton baptisms in Roberton Parish, three in Selkirk and one in Ettrick.

Prior to the unions of the crowns of England and Scotland, the Scottish Border was divided into three districts; the east, west and middle marches. Each march was presided over by a warden who settled disputes with the warden of the appropriate march in England, as Border warfare was rife at this time with frequent cattle raids. The Scotts of Buccleuch, one of the most powerful Border clans, were wardens of the Middle march, which included the Sheriffdom of Selkirk. By 1532 when the then warden, Sir Walter Scott, led an army of 3,000 strong into England it was the Scott family who owned the lands of Synton, not the Sintons. When the Sintons came to Ulster towards the end of the 17th century, they came as tenant farmers rather than landlords.

By 1700 the pattern, distribution, and frequency of the surnames of Ireland we know today was largely established.

From the early 18th century, a new feature was remarked on that was to have a very significant effect on the population make-up of the English-speaking countries of the world, namely emigration. At a conservative estimate 120,000 Presbyterians left the north of Ireland for the American colonies between 1718 and 1774. On the eve of the American Revolution over 30% of Pennsylvania's 350,000 inhabitants were of North Irish origins. A combination of bad harvests, exorbitant rents and the feelings of second-class citizenship in a country which they had defended on no less than three occasions in the 17th century drove many of them to a new life in North America.

Most Ulster immigrants in this period came out as indentured servants. In return for payment of their passage the emigrant signed an indenture agreeing to serve the owner of the ship for an agreed period. On arrival advertisements for their sale were placed in the local newspapers. In the 1770s indentured servants were being sold on board vessels in Philadelphia for 15 pounds for a term which varied from two to four years. The price of a horse was then 25 to 40 pounds!

By the 1830s emigration rather than land subdivision was seen as the answer to population growth. The population of Ireland could not be supported, owing to decline in the domestic linen industry and to increasing efforts by the landlords to improve their estates by enlarging farm sizes. The Famine opened the floodgates resulting in unparalleled emigration. Between 1846 and 1851 it is estimated one million Irish emigrated to the United States. Only 20% of this total left directly from Ireland; the port of Liverpool carried 75% of all Irish emigrants. New York received well over 60% of all Irish immigrants in these years.

Heavy emigration continued throughout the 19th century with the population of Ireland falling from 8,175,124 in 1841 to 4,458,775 in 1901. By 1981 the population of Ireland stood at 5,005,605.

The United States remained by far the most popular destination, but significant numbers of Irish also went to Canada, Australia, New Zealand and Great Britain. In the decade 1880 to 1889, 804,910 people emigrated from Ireland, of which 635,459 or 79% went to the U.S.A. Of the remainder, 48,084 or 6% went to England and Wales, 31,779 or 3.9% to Scotland, 41,321 or 5.1% to Canada, 39,168 or 4.9% to Australia and 5,950 or 0.7% to New Zealand.

In addition to free emigration, forced transportation of 30,000 men and 9,000 women from Ireland between 1791 and 1868 made a significant contribution to the Irish population in Australia. Transportation was the Georgian answer to the paranoia of the British ruling class to what they saw as the emergence of a "criminal class." Between 1614 and 1775, some 50,000 English convicts were deported to America. When the American colonies were removed as an outlet, Australia was selected as the new destination for Britain's and Ireland's criminals. For the first 50 years of its existence as a European settlement, Australia depended on convict labour, usually assigned to free settlers, to sustain economic growth. To a large extent the convicts were the pioneer settlers of Australia. They opened it up for the free, and often government-assisted, emigrants who started coming in substantial numbers from 1830, and in droves with the gold discoveries of 1851 in New South Wales and Victoria.

The end result is that there are now very substantial numbers of people of Irish origin in the U.S.A., Canada, Australia, New Zealand and Great Britain. According to the 1980 U.S. census, 43 million Americans, approximately 20% of her population, are of Irish origin. In the first half of the 19th century half-a-million Irish emigrants sailed for Canada, although approximately one-half of them made their way to the U.S.A. from there. Today 5 million Canadians, or 20% of her population, are of Irish descent. Five million Australians, or 30% of her population, and 450,000 New Zealanders, or 14% of her population, can claim Irish ancestry. By 1841 there were half a million Irish living in England, while between 1800 and 1850, 200,000 Irish migrated to Scotland. At a conservative estimate there are today over 7 million people with Irish origins in Great Britain.

This broad sweep of Irish history hopefully goes someway towards explaining why Irish ancestry is proclaimed with such great pride, not only within Ireland, but also in Great Britain, North America, Australia and New Zealand.

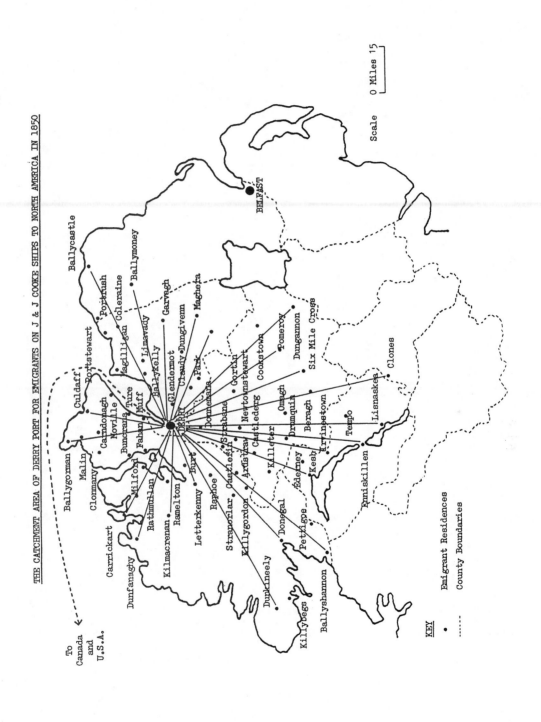

THE CATCHMENT AREA OF DERRY PORT FOR EMIGRANTS ON J & J COOKE SHIPS TO NORTH AMERICA IN 1850

To
Canada
and
U.S.A.

Ballycastle

Ballygorman
Culdaff
Malin
Clonmany
Carndonagh
Moville
Buncrana
Fahan
Bridge
Milford
Rathmullan
Carrickart
Dunfanaghy
Kilmacrenan
Ramelton
Letterkenny
Raphoe
Strabane
Castlefin
Killygordon
Donegal
Dunkineely
Pettigoe
Killybegs
Ballyshannon

Portrush
Coleraine
Ballymoney
Macilligan
Limavady
Ballykelly
Glendermot
Cready Dungiven
Park
Magheta
Garvagh

Portstewart

DERRY
Dornemana
Newtonstewart
Castlederg
Killeter
Adernoy
Kesh

BELFAST

Pomeroy
Dungannon
Six Mile Cross
Cookstown
Gortin
Omagh
Beragh
Irvinestown
Tempo
Enniskillen

Clones

Lisnaskea

KEY   • Emigrant Residences
         ---- County Boundaries

Scale   0 Miles 15

GETTING STARTED OVERSEAS

This chapter is intended for those people of Irish descent whose immediate ancestors have lived in those countries with large Irish communities, namely the United States of America, Canada, Australia, New Zealand and Great Britain. Many people in these countries make the mistake of believing that tracing their Irish roots begins in Ireland. It does not, it begins in their home county. It is only by building up a picture of your ancestors there that you will find the necessary clues to make a worthwhile search in Ireland.

Knowing that your ancestor came from Ireland is just not enough. Ideally you want to find out where in Ireland he came from, preferably a townland or parish address, the year he emigrated, the port he arrived at, his age on emigration, if he was married when he came out, and if so, the Christian name and maiden name of his wife and the names and ages of any children. In some cases family tradition may be able to provide answers to these questions, but in most cases various records will have to be searched for this information. It is, therefore, the intention of this section to give heart to those who think this is a daunting task by giving examples drawn from a variety of record sources in the various countries. It will show how clues can be built up on the origins of an Irish ancestor. Always remember when examining any record source that your purpose is essentially to extract information against three key words: NAME, LOCATION and DATE.

AUSTRALIA

Australia has, without a doubt, a superb collection of records for the genealogically minded. The three prime sources of convict records, assisted immigration lists, and birth, marriage and death certificates provide a wealth of relevant detail for those tracking down their Irish ancestor.

Convict indents, in which the convicts were listed by ship on their arrival in Sydney, date from 1788, i.e. form the earliest beginnings of the colony. The early indents give the name, date and place of conviction for every convict, while those from the 1820s also provide their native place and age. This detail on individual convicts can also be followed up in Ireland. For example, the report of the trial of Wilson Cornwall , who was sentenced to 15 years transportation at the Crown Court in Londonderry on Saturday, 23 March 1839, was recorded in the *Londonderry Sentinel* of 30 March 1839. Seemingly, Wilson Cornwall and an accomplice, Moses Hutchinson, robbed Alexander Mitchell, a linen merchant, of four bank notes together with all his silver coins, his great coat and umbrella, after they all had shared a few beers and a half glass of whiskey at Mr. Mann's public house in Castledawson, County Londonderry. In the transportation registers Wilson Cornwall's crime was classed as highway robbery. Prior to transportation, Wilson was held in the County Jail on Bishop Street in the city of Londonderry.

To entice the Irish emigrant to Australia, assisted passage was introduced. Lists of these immigrants date from 1828 and the information in them is very comprehensive. For example, in 1864 Thomas Connolly arrived at Sydney on board the ship *Serocco*. Thomas, aged 29, was a Roman Catholic and a policeman from Ballygar in County Galway. He could read and write, and his parents were Michael and Ellen Connolly, also of Ballygar. Thus, with this one entry you have all the information you need to trace the Connollys in Ireland.

Birth, marriage and death certificates, likewise provide an abundance of information. For example, from the New South Wales death certificate of Sarah Heathwood, who died on 3rd April 1936, aged 94 years, we can deduce the following information: Sarah was born in Ardarragh townland in Newry Parish, County Down around 1842: in 1867, aged 25 years, she married William Heathwood in County Roscommon, Her children, John born c. 1868, Robert 1869, Annie 1871, Richard 1874, and William 1876, were all born in Ireland. In 1877, the family emigrated to Queensland where another son, Joseph, was born in 1879. Sarah was buried on 4th April 1936 in the Presbyterian cemetery at Casino, New South Wales. A full family history can, therefore, be gleaned from this one certificate.

Gravestone inscriptions should also be searched. In the Catholic cemetery at Hartley, New South Wales, a tombstone erected by the police of Western District records that Thomas Madden, a constable born in County Mayo, was accidently shot dead at Pilpit Hill on 30 April 1867, aged 30.

NEW ZEALAND

Passenger lists in New Zealand, as in Australia, were kept at the port of arrival. The earliest are those for the New Zealand Company vessels, arriving at the ports of Wellington, Nelson, New Plymouth and Otago. These lists date from 1840 and provide the emigrant's name, age, occupation, wife's age and children's age and sex. New Zealand became a British colony only in 1840, when she was annexed to New South Wales. Passenger lists, therefore, go back to the earliest beginnings of the colony.

Before 1840, New Zealand had a very small European population. According to the *Derry Journal* of 18 February 1840, "With but few exceptions, the white population was composed of outcasts of Great Britain--runaway convicts, swindlers and thieves from New South Wales and Van Dieman's Land."

From 1853, New Zealand was administered by provincial governments at Canterbury, Wellington, Nelson, Auckland and Otago. Each province compiled passenger lists of varying quality.

Unfortunately, in both New Zealand and Australia census records were destroyed once the relevant statistical information had been extracted from them.

Civil registration of births and deaths commenced in 1848, but marriages were not recorded until 1855. In terms of identifying the Irish origins of an ancestor, death certificates are an extremely valuable source, especially after 1876. From that year the place of birth, the parents' names and the date and place of marriage of the deceased were recorded. Marriage certificates from 1880 are equally useful as they give the birthplace and parents' names of both bride and groom.

Parish registers of baptisms, marriages and burials, held locally by the clergymen, should be consulted for details on births, marriages and deaths before the commencement of civil registration.

UNITED STATES OF AMERICA

A New York genealogist, B-Ann Moorhouse, made use of federal and state censuses, marriage and death records, naturalization records, directories, passenger lists, probate records, cemetery inscriptions and death notices in newspapers to research 400 Irish-born and their descendants who resided in Brooklyn, New York during the 19th century. Regarding clues to place of origin in Ireland, she found death notices in the local Brooklyn newspapers of the time to be of most value, as they consistently gave the exact place of origin of the Irish-born. In another case, the will of William Ferguson, dated 1873, in mentioning a farm his sister had left to him in Ballygarvey in Rathaspick Parish, County Westmeath, identified the Irish origins of this Brooklyn merchant.

The U.S.A. has comprehensive passenger lists for ships arriving from 1820, but, unfortunately they provide only two clues relating to the origin of the emigrant--the port of departure of the ship and the nationality of the passenger. This is of limited value when it is realized that the vast majority of Irish emigrants in the 19th century sailed from Liverpool. The lists, however, give the name, occupation and age of the emigrant. It was not until 1893 and the Immigration Act that the former address in Ireland of an emigrant was recorded.

No official registers of passengers leaving Irish ports in the 19th century were kept except for a brief period, 1803-06. Among the business records of two Londonderry firms, J & J Cooke for the years 1847 to 1867, and William McCorkell & Co., 1863 to 1871, passenger lists recording the residence of 27,495 emigrants in Ireland have survived. The major destinations of the passengers carried by these firms were New York and Philadelphia in the U.S., and Quebec and St. John, New Brunswick in Canada. The Ordnance Survey compilers recorded the names, ages, religion and townland addresses of emigrants for many parishes in Counties Antrim and Londonderry for a few years during the period 1833 to 1839. Again, Canada and the U.S. were the major destinations of these emigrants. These two sources have now been indexed and published by the Genealogical Publishing Company of Baltimore.

In Colonial America the Land Patent Books of Virginia, the registers of indentured servants in Pennsylvania, and petitions for land grants in Maryland and South Carolina identify many recently arrived immigrants.

A census has been taken every ten years in the U.S. since 1790, and from 1850 the returns provide the country of birth and age of all members of the household, not just the head of household.

Tombstone inscriptions should be sought out. In St. Mary's Cemetery in Lee, Massachusetts, the following inscription can be found: "John Dooley, a native of the town of Leabeg, parish of Ferbane, King's County, died August 14 1863 aged 53 years." King's County is now renamed Offaly.

Naturalization records are another useful source. On April 1839, for example, John Austin aged 26, giving his place of birth as County Leitrim, declared his intention before Franklin County Court at St. Albans, Vermont to become a U.S. citizen.

CANADA

As passenger lists for Canada are rare, this makes the business records of Cooke and McCorkell and the emigrant lists in the Ordnance Survey memoirs (both described previously) very valuable indeed. Lists of arrivals at Halifax and Quebec were kept from 1865.

In 1895, after it was noted that 40% of all passengers arriving in Canada were actually bound for the U.S., a system of joint inspection of immigrants coming overland from Canada was established. From 1847, the two ports of Portland and Falmouth, Maine were becoming increasingly popular as ports of entry for Irish immigrants coming down from Quebec and the Maritime Provinces to the U.S. In these cases, therefore, Irish immigrants leaving Canada for the U.S.A. will be noted.

In the absence of passenger lists the best hope of linking an ancestor to his place of origin in Ireland may lie in the identification of a marriage entry of a newly-arrived immigrant in a church register. Frequently, the marriage registers give the county of birth in Ireland, and occasionally, the exact place of origin of bride and groom. In the years 1801 to 1845, for example, the weddings of 3,000 Irish immigrants, giving their parents' names and native parishes, were recorded in Halifax, Nova Scotia.

Land grants can be extremely useful in identifying recent immigrants. To obtain land from the Colonial government and, after 1867 from the Provincial authorities, a settler had to make a formal application, known as a petition, in which details on place of origin, date of arrival in Canada, name of wife and children and their ages are often given. There exists a computerized Land Records Index for the years 1780 to 1914 with two alphabetical listings, one by applicant's name and one by township.

As in other provinces, gravestone inscriptions can prove very enlightening. For example, in Barkerville cemetery in Barkerville, British Columbia, one of the tombstones reads, "In memory of Patrick McKenna, native of Duleek, County Meath, Ireland, Died June 2, 1914 aged 59."

Death notices in newspapers should also be sought out. *The Herald*, the local newspaper of Charlottetown, Prince Edward Island, on 3 July 1867 carried the following death notice, "On Monday June 3rd at his residence, Monaghan Settlement Lot 36, James Trainor, aged 80 years. The deceased was a native of the parish of Donah, townland of Strawmore, County Monaghan, Ireland and emigrated to this island in the year 1835, May he rest in peace."

GREAT BRITAIN

Civil registration of births, marriages and deaths began in England and Wales in 1837 and in Scotland in 1855. Despite providing much genealogical information of great value, they give no clue to the former residence of those who were born in Ireland. The marriage entries in church records, however, will provide the Irish origins of bride and groom. For example, the register of St. Vincent de Paul in Liverpool on 4 June 1862, records the marriage of Joseph Edward Huges of Sligo to Sarah Quin of 13 Moore Place, London Road.

From 1841, census returns in both England and Scotland list all members of the household, together with their ages and occupations. Furthermore, they will identify those people who were born in Ireland. In Scotland, from 1851, the specific town or parish of birth is given.

Gravestone inscriptions and death notices in newspapers will probably provide the best means of identifying a more precise Irish address of an ancestor. In Clifton Parish churchyard, Bristol, there can be found the following gravestone inscriptions: "Mary Clutterbuck of Derryhusker, County Tipperary, Ireland, died 17 December 1847, aged 99 years." And in the *Bristol Journal* of Saturday, 21 January 1837, the following death notice was reported: "January 14 at Royal York Crescent, Clifton, Robert Eyre Purdon Coote Esqr., of Ballyclough, County Cork."

Hopefully, all these examples show that much can be done in the home country to identify as precisely as possible the names of ancestors who emigrated from Ireland; their age, so that an approximate date of birth can be estimated; where they lived in Ireland and their religious denomination. Armed with this information, you can then begin to plan your trip to Ireland.

FIRST STEPS

The first, and perhaps the most crucial, step in compiling your family tree is probably the one most people neglect: namely the quizzing of relations and family friends. It is too often assumed that genealogy means looking through dusty parish registers that haven't seen the light of day in years or walking through overgrown cemeteries in search of an ancestor's gravestone; in other words, a total reliance on the written word. People who do this are not only missing out on a vital source of information but also on one of the joys of genealogy. The information and anecdotes relatives can provide help bring the family tree to life, as well as providing much needed clues for its construction. The oral tradition within the family circle is of immense value.

Having made the decision to research your family tree, now is the time to get in touch with those relatives you haven't seen in ages. Parents, grandparents, uncles and aunts should all be questioned. Names, places, dates and any anecdotes, no matter how unlikely or inaccurate you might think them to be, associated with all branches of your family tree should be recorded. In genealogy, you never know when a piece of information that seemed irrelevant might, on reflection, suggest a line of inquiry.

The memories and knowledge of the elderly should not be underestimated. The McCook family story, as described in the first chapter, was built on the knowledge of 87-year-old Robert Graham. In my case, I have two 80-year-old great aunts who can remember as young girls sitting with their grandmother, listening to the stories she told them. It was through their recollections that I was able to trace the English origins of the Metcalfes of Lurgan, County Armagh. They were able to tell me that George Metcalfe, my great grandfather, came from Headington in Oxfordshire in the 19th century to set up a poultry business in Lurgan. The registers of Headington Parish church confirmed this. On 12 April 1840, George was baptized, his parents being George Metcalfe and Mary Wake. According to the 1841 census, George was a blacksmith and a gun maker and the family lived at Church Lane in Headington. Without the oral tradition, the identification of George Metcalfe's birthplace would have been a more difficult task. The 1901 census return for George, however, giving his age as 60 and his birthplace as Oxfordshire, does provide sufficient information to justify a search through the indexes to the English registers of births, which commence from 1837. The moral being, if one avenue closes its doors to you, search for another.

In one interesting case, a lady who came into our centre was attempting to trace her own name, which was a rather unusual one, Tarleton. The oral tradition passed down in the family is that the Tarletons came to County Offaly from Liverpool in the 16th century. Tarleton is indeed a Lancashire name, as the surname is derived from a place of that name in the County. Furthermore, history records when Mary Tudor came to the throne of England in 1553, land which had been confiscated from the O'Mores and O'Connors of Counties Laois and Offaly was planted by settlers from England. These counties were then renamed Queen's and King's County. It seems the Tarletons came over with this plantation. The Householders Index to the Griffiths Valuation and Tithe Applotment Books for County Offaly seems to confirm this, inasmuch as in the early 19th century Tarleton households could be found in Ballykean, Geashill, Killoughy and Kilmanaghan parishes, with a concentration in the parish of Geashill, especially.

In addition to oral tradition, a search should be made

through family papers to unearth old photographs, newspaper clippings with perhaps an obituary, letters, or even a family bible with its own family tree within. You never know until you look, what useful information may be lurking in the back of a cupboard or hiding in a box in the attic.

You will soon find that you have amassed a lot of information which needs to be organized to prevent it from becoming unwieldy. The simplest and most effective method is a pedigree chart on which you can record details of direct line ancestors. A pedigree chart ("Family Tree") for the recording of up to four generations is enclosed with this book. Make as many photocopies of it as you require. Against "Family Tree," enter the surname of the family line being traced. Against "You," enter your own name or the name of the ancestor being traced. Then fill in the full names of parents, grandparents and great grandparents. For each name enter their date and place of birth, marriage and death. Information that is unknown is simply left blank, thus highlighting those areas where further research is needed. The chart will be constantly updated as new information comes to light.

This pedigree chart is ideal for those recording all family lines, but it offers no space for detailing collateral ancestors, i.e. the brothers and sisters of direct line ancestors and their descendants. This is easily overcome by drawing up your own pedigree chart in which there are no limitations to its size. For example, on a roll of paper with dimensions of 15 feet by 2 feet deep a relative has drawn up a family tree which identifies all offspring from my great grandparents George Mitchell and Margaret Jane Patton and their eleven children.

The conventions in drawing up your own pedigree chart are straightforward. Start at the top of the page with the ancestor whose descendants you want to record and link him to his wife with the recognized marriage symbol of "=". From this marriage symbol, draw a vertical line to join a horizontal line whose length is determined by the number of children attached to it by other short vertical lines. The same procedure is followed for any other marriages amongst these children. Children should be listed in order of birth, but in some circumstances it is an advantage to change the order so as to fit the requirements of your chart design. The following standard symbols and abbreviations should be used: "b." for born, "c." about, "m." married, "d." died, "?" if uncertain of accuracy of information and blank spaces for information which is not yet known. An example of such a pedigree chart, drawn up to present the McCook Family history described previously, is shown below.

Note how people of the same generation are kept on the same level. In this case, two sets of cousins are displayed with John's sons being born in New Zealand and Archibald's in Ireland. The great advantage with such a chart is that you choose what families to highlight. In our example it is the families of Archibald and John.

With this type of pedigree chart, it is perhaps best to draw up a rough draft to ensure all issue you want to include can be accommodated, as such charts lose their visual attractiveness and clarity if you continually add to them. Our chart would have to be redesigned if we wanted to include the children of Robert, the youngest son of Alexander McCook. For those with artistic flair, their pedigree charts could become the focus of considerable attention and envy!

FAMILY TREE

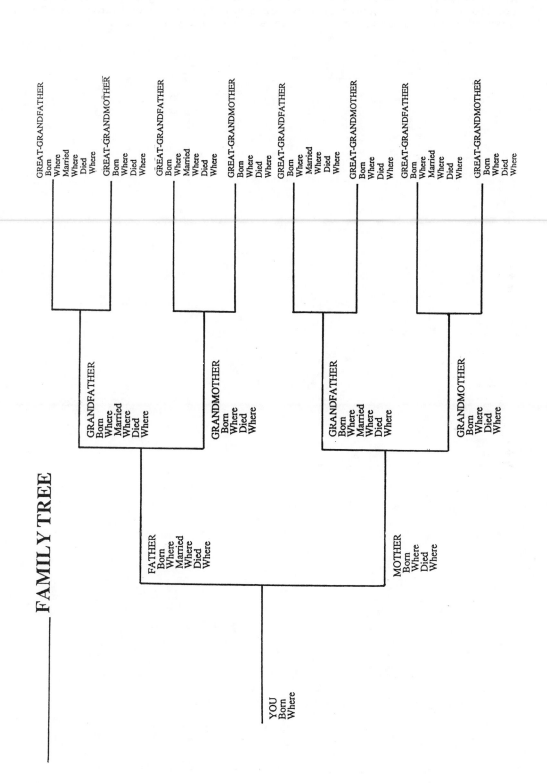

YOU
Born
Where

FATHER
Born
Where
Married
Where
Died
Where

MOTHER
Born
Where
Died
Where

GRANDFATHER
Born
Where
Married
Where
Died
Where

GRANDMOTHER
Born
Where
Died
Where

GRANDFATHER
Born
Where
Married
Where
Died
Where

GRANDMOTHER
Born
Where
Died
Where

GREAT-GRANDFATHER
Born
Where
Married
Where
Died
Where

GREAT-GRANDMOTHER
Born
Where
Died
Where

GREAT-GRANDFATHER
Born
Where
Married
Where
Died
Where

GREAT-GRANDMOTHER
Born
Where
Died
Where

GREAT-GRANDFATHER
Born
Where
Married
Where
Died
Where

GREAT-GRANDMOTHER
Born
Where
Died
Where

GREAT-GRANDFATHER
Born
Where
Married
Where
Died
Where

GREAT-GRANDMOTHER
Born
Where
Died
Where

By the time you've visited or written to all your relatives, located any old family documents and recorded all this information on pedigree charts, you should have built up an outline family tree detailing names, locations and dates. Only now should you consider searching the seven major record sources outlined in the next chapter to confirm, fill in and extend your family tree.

McCOOK FAMILY TREE - IRELAND, AUSTRALIA AND NEW ZEALAND

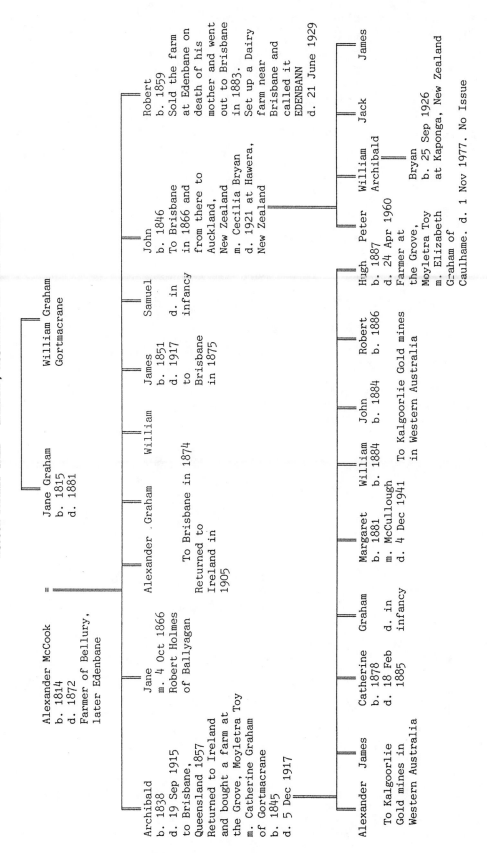

Alexander McCook
b. 1814
d. 1872
Farmer of Bellury,
later Edenbane

=

Jane Graham
b. 1815
d. 1881

William Graham
Gortmacrane

Archibald
b. 1838
d. 19 Sep 1915
to Brisbane,
Queensland 1857
Returned to Ireland
and bought a farm at
the Grove, Moyletra Toy
m. Catherine Graham
of Gortmacrane
b. 1845
d. 5 Dec 1917

Jane
m. 4 Oct 1866
Robert Holmes
of Ballyagan

Alexander .Graham

To Brisbane in 1874
Returned to
Ireland in
1905

William

Samuel

d. in
infancy

James
b. 1851
d. 1917
to
Brisbane
in 1875

John
b. 1846
To Brisbane
in 1866 and
from there to
Auckland,
New Zealand
m. Cecilia Bryan
d. 1921 at Hawera,
New Zealand

Robert
b. 1859
Sold the farm
at Edenbane on
death of his
mother and went
out to Brisbane
in 1883.
Set up a Dairy
farm near
Brisbane and
called it
EDENBANN
d. 21 June 1929

Alexander James

To Kalgoorlie
Gold mines in
Western Australia

Catherine
b. 1878
d. 18 Feb
1885

Graham

d. in
infancy

Margaret
b. 1881
m. McCullough
d. 4 Dec 1941

William
b. 1884

John
b. 1884

To Kalgoorlie Gold mines
in Western Australia

Robert
b. 1886

Hugh
b. 1887
d. 24 Apr 1960
Farmer at
the Grove,
Moyletra Toy
m. Elizabeth
G=aham of
Caulhame. d. 1 Nov 1977. No Issue

Peter

William
Archibald

Jack

James

Bryan
b. 25 Sep 1926
at Kaponga, New Zealand

MAJOR RECORD SOURCES

I have found, during my twenty years in genealogy both as a tutor and manager of a Genealogy Centre, that the seven record sources examined in this section will enable you to build up a detailed family tree stretching back six or seven generations. The records being civil registers, parish registers, gravestone inscriptions, wills, the 1901 or 1911 census, and Griffiths Valuation and Tithe Applotment Books. To make the text less cluttered, fuller details on the administrative divisions and record offices, which will be constantly referred to in this section, are contained in the glossaries at the back of the book. Refer to the glossaries whenever you feel you need more detail. For each record source is included a description, detail on how to make best use of the record, and suggestions for using the information it contains to further your research.

CIVIL REGISTRATION

Civil registration in Ireland of births, deaths and Roman Catholic marriages didn't commence until January 1864. Protestant marriages, however, were subject to registration from April 1845. For the purpose of registration, Ireland was divided into about 800 registrars' districts, which were grouped into 140 poor law unions. The registrar of the union was responsible for collecting the registrations made by his district registrars and returning the lot to the Registrar General in Dublin, where complete indexes covering the whole country were compiled.

The detail included in the birth, marriage and death certificates, together with the indexes, help to make them an ideal starting point in researching ancestors who were born, married or died after the commencement of civil registration.

A birth certificate provides the name, date of birth and place of birth of the child, together with the father's name, occupation, and residence and the mother's name and maiden name.

A marriage certificate gives the names, ages, occupations and residences of the bride and groom, together with the names and occupations of their fathers. The date and place of marriage and the names of the two witnesses are also included.

A death certificate gives the deceased's name, age, occupation, cause of death, and place of death.

The certificates, therefore, vary in the amount and usefulness of information provided. Death certificates offer the minimum of information and, in many cases, are only useful as a means to get an approximate date of birth of an ancestor, from the age given at death. A birth certificate, on the other hand, provides detail on three ancestors, namely father, mother, and child. A marriage certificate is perhaps the most useful, as it provides information on four direct ancestors and two branches of the family tree, i.e. the bride's and groom's lines. By giving the addresses of both bride and groom at the time of their marriage, it may be possible to identify two ancestral homes.

Owing to the limited information provided in the indexes, it would be very difficult to identify an ancestor, especially one with a common surname, without fairly precise information to the date and location of the event. The early indexes were compiled annually, but with increasing numbers of entries, they soon had to be arranged by the quarter year. Furthermore, the only

BIRTH CERTIFICATE

Index: Mitchell Samuel Patton, Londonderry   Vol 17 page 217 Year 1868

1868 Births registered in the District of Killea in the Union of Londonderry in the County of Donegal

No	Date and Place of Birth	Name	Sex	Name and Surname and Dwelling Place of Father	Name and Surname & Maiden Surname of Mother	Rank or Profession of Father	Signature, Qualification and Residence of Informant	When Registered
	Twenty second September 1868 Colehill All Saints	Samuel	Male	George Mitchell Colehill	Margaret Jane Mitchell Formerly Patton	School Master	George Mitchell Father Colehill	3rd Oct 1868

guidance to the address is the poor law union name in which the event was registered. Before using the indexes, therefore, you need to identify the union or unions associated with your ancestors. You can do this by making use of a book called *THE GENERAL ALPHABETICAL INDEX TO THE TOWNLANDS AND TOWNS, PARISHES AND BARONIES OF IRELAND*, better known as "The Townland Index," which can be found in many libraries. This book will identify the poor law union for all of Ireland's 60,462 townlands.

With such limited information in the indexes, a birth or death will be hard to identify without a fairly clear idea of when and where it happened. As the marriage indexes list both parties, there is a cross-referencing system which may enable the identification of a marriage in the absence of both an address and date.

Examples of a birth, marriage and death certificate, together with the appropriate entries in the indexes are shown overleaf. They demonstrate very nicely how a family tree can be built up using a series of certificates. The following family tree can be drawn up from the three certificates:

```
George Mitchell                      William Patton
Schoolmaster                         Farmer
       :                             Carrickanany, Co. Armagh
       :                                      :
George Mitchell           =          Margaret Jane Patton
                          :
m. 8 Jan 1853             :
at Balleek, Co. Armagh    :
Schoolmaster and          :
Petty Sessions Clerk      :
d. 4 Apr 1901             :
at Mormeal, Co. L'Derry   :
                          :
           Samuel Patton Mitchell
           b. 22 Sep 1868 at Colehill, Co. Donegal
```

The information contained in birth, marriage and death certificates provides many clues on which to base further research. In our example, the following steps could be followed up: the search of relevant church registers at Balleek and Colehill for Patton and Mitchell baptisms, respectively; a visit to the graveyards around Colehill, Carrickanany and Mormeal; the identification of George Mitchell's will, as we know he died in 1901; a search of the 1901 census returns for Mormeal, as they were recorded just a few days before George died; and a look through the Griffiths Valuation for Mitchells at Colehill and Pattons at Carrickanany.

In searching out relevant certificates, there are four main offices to be considered: the Registrar General's Offices in Belfast and Dublin and the local registrar offices of Northern Ireland and Eire. Information on the registers they hold, hours of opening and fees are listed in the glossary. Certificates can be purchased by post, assuming you can provide sufficient information to identify them. The staff in these offices will not carry out research on your behalf.

MARRIAGE CERTIFICATE

Index: Mitchell George, Newry   Vol 8 Page 510 Year 1853

         Patton Margaret Jane, Newry   Vol 8 Page 510 Year 1853

1853 Marriage solemnised at Balleek Church in the Parish of Balleek in the County of Armagh

No	When married	Name and Surname	Age	Condition	Rank or profession	Residence at the time of marriage	Father's name and Surname	Rank or Profession of father
	8th January 1853	George Mitchell	of age	Bachelor	Schoolmaster	All Saints, Donegal	George Mitchell	School-master
		Margaret Jane Patton	of age	Spinster	-----	Carrickananny	William Patton	Farmer

Married in the Parish church of Balleek according to the Rites and Ceremonies of the United Church of England and Ireland by me

Charles Crossler

in the presence of us Henry Devlin

John Patton

24

PARISH REGISTERS

Before civil registration baptism, marriage and burial details of an ancestor will have to be found in parish registers. The identification of an ancestor in these records will require careful preparation. Unlike the civil registers there is no national index to church registers, but the rewards from using this source are well worth the effort.

Before seeking out church records you will need to know where your ancestors lived and their religious denomination, as Ireland has a complex parish structure. The Church of Ireland and Roman Catholic churches have an all-Irish parish structure, the former because of its privileged position, before 1870, as the established church, and the latter because of its numerical strength. The Church of Ireland parish largely coincides with the boundaries of the civil parish and retains the civil parish name, while the Catholic church does not correspond with either the names or boundaries of the civil parishes. The Presbyterian church doesn't have a parish structure as such, with the congregations generally forming where there was sufficient demand from local Presbyterian families. In those areas with a high Presbyterian population, there could be many Presbyterian meeting houses. For example, the civil parish of Ballymore in County Armagh had six Presbyterian congregations by the middle of the 19th century. By contrast, in County Wicklow, with 57 civil parishes, there was only one Presbyterian Congregation--at Bray. The other Protestant dissenting denominations such as Methodists, Baptists, Congregationalists and Quakers, formed where there were enough like-minded people.

After identifying the religious affiliation of your ancestor and their residence, you need to identify what church registers exist for your area and their dates of commencement. In the case of the Church of Ireland, many of their registers do not survive, for of 1,006 pre-1870 registers deposited in the Public Record Office, Dublin, all but four were burnt in the fire there in 1922. Despite the fire, many registers of great age have survived. For example, in County Dublin seventeen Church of Ireland registers with commencement dates between 1619 and 1699 and twenty between 1700 and 1799 survive.

One feature of the Presbyterian church is the concentration of congregations within relatively small areas. Doctrinal differences and disagreement over a choice of ministers often divided the original congregation and led to the creation of a new one. This 19th-century growth of Presbyterian congregations in Ulster may mean two or three registers will have to be searched, even if you know the exact area your ancestor lived in. It is also very possible for the baptism, marriage and burial records of Protestant dissenters to be within the registers of the Church of Ireland, as for centuries the established church claimed the right to administer baptism, marriage and burial ceremonies to all Protestants.

In the case of the Roman Catholic church, the Penal Laws resulted in the late erection of chapels in many parishes and the late commencement of many registers. Of the 41 Catholic parishes serving the 52 civil parishes of County Donegal, 29 of them have registers that don't commence until after 1850. The Catholic registers, however, in the bigger cities can be of an early date. There are baptism and marriage records for Wexford Town dating back to 1671. Waterford has four parishes whose registers date back to the 1700s.

25

DEATH CERTIFICATE

Index: 1901 June Quarter   Mitchell George, Magherafelt   Vol 1 page 601

1901 Deaths registered in the District of Maghera in the Union of Magherafelt in the County of Londonderry

No	Date and Place of Death	Name and Surname	Sex	Condition	Age last Birthday	Rank, Profession or occupation	Certified cause of death and duration of illness	Signature, qualification and residence of informant	When registered
	1901 Fourth April Mormeal	George Mitchell	Male	Widower	73 years	Clerk of Petty Sessions (Retired)	Age and Influenza fourteen days certified	John Mitchell son Mormeal	13th April 1901

A general reference book such as *A Guide to Irish Parish Registers*, by the author (Genealogical Publishing Company, Baltimore, 1988), will identify the registers of all denominations which survive for any area in Ireland you are interested in. It will also give their earliest commencement date. The National Archives, Dublin and Public Record Office, Belfast hold more detailed lists of surviving registers and their commencement dates. These offices also hold copies of many church registers. The National Library, Dublin has microfilm copies of all Catholic registers. The original registers of all denominations are, in most cases, held locally by the clergy.

Having decided on a register to search, you will have to resist the impulse to glance quickly through the pages, stopping only briefly at those surnames which you think might belong to your ancestors. The registers, especially of a later date, may be tabulated and the information written in the appropriate columns, neatly and legibly. But often the information is simply written, and not too clearly at that, in sentence form. The implications for the impatient will be to overlook the very entry you are looking for.

With hand-written records there is always the possibility of misreading surnames. To complicate matters further are the numerous spelling variations to be found of the same name. Uniformity in spelling surnames is really a phenomenon of the 20th century. The clergy, in entering relevant details, often had to write down names based on pronunciation, as many people could not write down or spell their name. This diversity was perpetuated by the fact that there were no recognized standards for spelling surnames.

On identifying a likely name in a register, which is spelt slightly differently from the name you are looking for, ask yourself if it is merely a spelling variation of the same name or a completely different name. The Thurles Parish indexing project in County Tipperary found, for example, that it was often difficult to distinguish Phelan from Whelan, Bourke from Rourke and Kelly from Kiely in their registers. The anglicization of the gaelic can also cause problems. For example, the surname Flood can be a mistranslation of the gaelic name Tully. In the Thurles registers, both names, Tully and Flood, frequently occur.

The patience and care taken in searching church registers is well worth it. You may be very fortunate and be able to follow successive generations back in time:

SHANKILL PARISH, COUNTY ARMAGH (CHURCH OF IRELAND)

Baptism Register

July 11 1824 Henry of parents Henry and May Corner of Lurgan

Marriage Register

April 23 1844 Henry Corner of Toberhuney in this parish, bachelor and Letitia Mathews of Cornreaney in the Parish of Donaghcloney, Spinster. By license.

A family tree can be drawn:

```
                    Henry Corner    =    May
                    of Toberhewny   ¦

                    Henry Corner       =    Letitia Mathews
                    bap. 11 Jul 1824        of Cornreaney
                    m. 23 Apr 1844
```

Like civil registers, because of their similar nature, the information from baptism, marriage and burial registers on names, dates, places and family connections can provide pointers to other record sources. In our example the marriage register identified two ancestral homes, namely Toberhewny townland, County Armagh and Cornreaney townland, County Down. The local graveyards can, therefore, be identified and visited. We can quickly search the tithe books, Griffiths Valuation and 1901 or 1911 census returns for Toberhewny and Cornreaney to identify Corner and Mathews households, respectively. These two townlands are in the poor law union of Lurgan, so the indexes to the civil registers could be searched for Corner and Mathews entries listed against Lurgan.

Of major significance for those researching parish registers has been the establishment of the **Irish Genealogical Project**. It is the intention of the Irish Genealogical Project (established in 1990), through a network of indexing centres, to computerise the major civil and church sources. Each area, usually a county, will have a specific centre, which will create a comprehensive genealogical database for their locality.

A database of course is only as good as the information it holds - if data is entered incorrectly or just simply does not exist in the first place there is nothing a computer can do to rectify this. The absence of relevant records is a well-known problem in Irish genealogy as many records were either destroyed or simply not kept until quite late on.

The addresses and contact name and telephone number of the centres set up, under the auspices of the Irish Genealogical Project, are listed in the glossary. Why not contact the appropriate centre to see if they can help you with your research.

The International Genealogical Index (IGI), compiled by the Mormans, could also be checked. Since 1961, the Church of Jesus Christ of Latter Day Saints, as part of its record extraction program, have computerized some Irish parish registers. The consolidated surname index thus created is made available on microfiche and can be consulted at their Family History Centres. For example, the registers for County Limerick, indexed and included in the IGI, are the Church of Ireland parishes of Ahascragh, Ardrahan and Athenry, and the Catholic registers of Ahascragh and Killian and Killeroran. The IGI now includes some Irish civil registration records, births from 1864 to 1874 and marriages 1845 to 1850, 1855, 1863 and 1864.

GRAVESTONE INSCRIPTIONS

With civil registration of births and deaths commencing in 1864, and with the patchy survival of church records before this time, gravestone inscriptions take on a special significance. Many Church of Ireland burial registers were destroyed by fire in the Public Record Office, Dublin in 1922, while the registers of the Catholic and Presbyterian churches are especially poor regarding burial entries. In many cases, therefore, a gravestone will be the only record of an ancestor's death. But gravestones offer much more than just the date of death of an ancestor. They frequently mention their residence and age on death, thus providing an approximate birth date. Many graves are family plots and the gravestone will record the deaths of more than one person. The gravestone located in First Garvagh Presbyterian graveyard, which played its part in unravelling the McCook family story, illustrates very nicely just how much information can be gleaned from an inscription:

In memory of Alexander McCook
who died in the year 1872, aged 58 years
and of his wife Jane who died in the year
1881, aged 66 years
his son Archibald McCook died 19 September
1915, aged 77 years
his wife Catherine died 5 December 1917 aged 72 years
Their children
Catherine died 18 February 1885 aged 7 years
Graham died in infancy and their daughter
Margaret McCullough died 4 December 1941 aged 60 years
Hugh died 24 April 1960 aged 73 years
Mary died 11 August 1963 aged 90 years
Elizabeth, wife of Hugh died 1 November
1977 aged 79 years.

From this inscription, the following family tree stretching over three generations can be drawn:

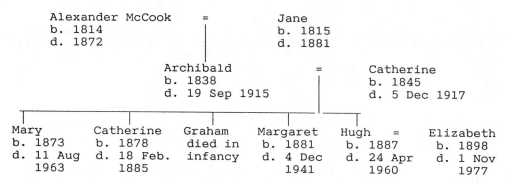

The identification of a gravestone will open many avenues for further research. Taking our example, the civil registers could be searched for the birth certificates of Archibald's children; the baptisms of Archibald and his father, Alexander, could be looked for in the baptism registers of First Garvagh Presbyterian Church, which commence from 1795; death certificates could be easily procured and in the case of Alexander McCook and his wife, they would provide their exact dates of death; the 1901 census should record Archibald and his family, while a will of Archibald McCook, if he made one, should be an easy matter to identify, as we know his date of death.

Clearly, on identifying an ancestor's residence, the local graveyards should be visited. The Ordnance Survey maps, at a scale of six inches to one mile, with the earliest edition dating back to the 1830s, should be consulted at your local library to identify all possible graveyards. With the establishment of new churches throughout the 19th century, many graveyards attached to the old church fell into disuse and can be easily overlooked.

Church of Ireland graveyards should be examined irrespective of an ancestor's religion. It was October 1829 before a Catholic cemetery opened in Dublin at Goldenbridge. Prior to the 1820s, owing to the operation of the Penal Laws, both Catholics and Protestants shared the same graveyards. And prior to the Burial Act of 1868, which permitted dissenting ministers to conduct burial services, the Church of Ireland clergy held jurisdiction over funeral services for all Protestants. Right up to the mid-19th century, it is not uncommon to find Presbyterian ministers and Methodist preachers buried in a Church of Ireland cemetery.

Unfortunately, the unkept state of many graveyards and the weathering of headstones precludes the reading of many inscriptions. It is not unusual to be able to read clearly an inscription of the 18th century incised on hard Welsh slate, while those of the late 19th century, on soft limestone and sandstone headstones, have been eroded away.

The importance of gravestone inscriptions to the genealogist can be seen in the increasing number of projects to transcribe them. Many Heritage Centres are copying the gravestones in their local area. The Ulster Historical Foundation, for example, under the direction of Professor Richard Clarke, has copied 200 graveyards, totalling 20,000 gravestones in County Down alone.

WILLS

Wills, with their tendency to list surviving relatives--brothers, sisters, children and even grandchildren--are very important documents. It may be possible, from a will, to draw up a family tree covering up to three generations. The only limitation being the small percentage of the population--usually the better off, such as gentry, farmers and merchants--who made wills. But don't let this deter you, as a substantial proportion of the population in the 19th century were tenant farmers. And from the year 1858, wills become relatively easy to identify.

Prior to 1858, ecclesiastical courts of the Church of Ireland, based in each diocese, were responsible for all matters of probate. Unfortunately, the original will books of these diocesan courts were largely destroyed in the fire in Dublin in 1922. The indexes, however, have survived, and furthermore, copies of many of these wills can be found in the National Archives, Dublin and Public Record Office, Belfast among the collections of family papers they hold. Always check the name indexes in these two offices, as they may hold an ancestor's will.

The Court of Probate and Letters of Administration Act (Ireland) 1857, transferred testamentary jurisdiction to a principal registry in Dublin and eleven district registries covering the remainder of the county. The significance of 1858 for the genealogist is not so much the change in authority for all matters of probate, but rather the appearance of printed volumes called calendars, which make it a simple task to identify wills proven and administrations granted. The calendars, compiled annually in alphabetical order by surname and christian name, give the name, address and occupation of the deceased, the place and date of death, together with the names and addresses of their executors. A full set of calendars can be found in the National Archives, Dublin and Public Record Office, Belfast and in the district registry offices.

The original wills were destroyed in the fire in 1922, but copies of the probated wills were also kept in the district registries and these are now deposited in the National Archives and Public Record Office. Belfast holds the will books for the districts of Belfast, Armagh and Londonderry, and Dublin has the books for the remaining eight districts. There are, unfortunately, no copies of wills probated in the principal registry in Dublin before 1922.

As a matter of course, if you know the exact date or approximate date of death of your ancestor, and if he died after 1858, you should check the calendars. In some cases, probate was taken out long after the date of death, so you should check at least ten calendars, i.e. ten years, after the death date before assuming your ancestor made no will. As you can quickly check through many calendars, I sometimes use them as a means to identify the date of death of a person, as opposed to the indexes to the civil registers of deaths.

The information you can expect to obtain from the calendar of wills and from a will itself is shown below:

CALENDAR OF WILLS 1898

MADDEN William — 25 April. Probate of the will of William Madden late of Gartenane County Cavan Farmer who died 28 November 1897 granted at CAVAN to James Bradshaw of the Manse Irvinestown County Fermanagh Wesleyan Minister and James Graham of Bailieborough County Cavan Merchant. Effects L589 6 shillings.

THE WILL

"I William Madden of Gartenane in the County of Cavan Farmer hereby revoke all former wills codicils and testamentary instruments heretofore made by me and declare this to be my last will and testament[.] I appoint the Reverend James Bradshaw formerly of the Manse Bailieborough in the County of Cavan and now of the Manse Irvinestown in the County of Fermanagh Wesleyan Minister and Mr James G Graham of Bailieborough in the County of Cavan Merchant to be the executors of this my will and I direct my said executors to pay my just debts and funeral and testamentary expenses[.] I confirm the gift which I have already made to my son Allen Madden of the farm upon which he now resides together with the dwelling and buildings thereon and the furniture live and dead agricultural stock crop implements of husbandry and other effects within or about or belonging to the said farm dwelling house or buildings[.] I give and bequeath to my wife Eliza Madden the sum of One Hundred pounds[.] I give and bequeath to my daughter Mary Jane Campbell the sum of Forty pounds[.] I give and bequeath to my daughter Annie Eliza Anderson the sum of Forty pounds[.] I give and bequeath to my son the aforesaid Allen Madden the sum of Sixty pounds[.] I give and bequeath to my daughter Margaret Burns the sum of Sixty pounds[.] I give and bequeath to my daughter Rebecca Young now resident in Sydney the sum of Twenty pounds[.] I give and bequeath to my daughter Fanny Madden the sum of Forty pounds[.] I give and bequeath to my daughter Georgia Anderson the sum of Twenty pounds[.] I give and bequeath to my daughter Jemima Madden the sum of Twenty pounds . . . In witness whereof I have set my hand to this my will the 17th day of November 1897 William Madden Gartanean[.]"

31

You should note that the will names William's wife and his eight children. It gives the married names of his daughters, together with the information that one of them, Rebecca, was living in Sydney, Australia. With this information the following family tree can be drawn up:

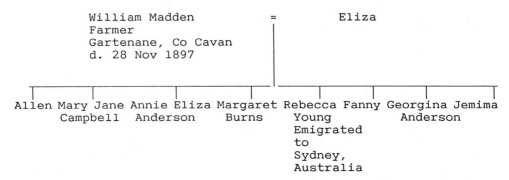

William Madden = Eliza
Farmer
Gartenane, Co Cavan
d. 28 Nov 1897

Allen Mary Jane Annie Eliza Margaret Rebecca Fanny Georgina Jemima
       Campbell   Anderson   Burns   Young   Anderson
                                          Emigrated
                                          to
                                          Sydney,
                                          Australia

Further research can now be successfully carried out based on this will: the 1901 census for Gartenane, County Craven should be examined; the graveyards in the area should be checked; if the ages of William's children can be obtained from these two sources, then birth certificates or baptism entries can be searched for, depending on whether they were born before or after 1864; a death certificate, which will give William's age, could be easily obtained; the Tithe Applotment Book and Griffiths Valuation for Bailieborough parish can be searched to see if the Maddens were farming there in the early and mid-19th century respectively, as the Townland Index locates Gartnaneane, the recognized spelling of the townland by the Ordnance Survey, in this parish.

THE 1901 AND 1911 CENSUS

Although census enumerations were carried out every decade from 1821, the earliest surviving complete return for all Ireland is that of 1901 and is complemented by that of 1911. Both returns give, for each member of the household, their name, age, religion, education, i.e. if they could read or write, occupation, marital status, county or city of birth and if a speaker of Irish.

The 1911 census provides additional information on the marriage, namely the number of years married, the number of children born and the number still living. Because of the very similar nature of the information contained, an examination of either the 1901 or 1911 census will be sufficient for most people's research needs.

As the two examples show, there is a wealth of very relevant information in the 1901 and 1911 census returns.

We can deduce from the 1901 census return that Dominick Timothy was born about 1848 and his wife Bridget c. 1851. There were nine children living at home with birth dates ranging from 1878 to 1894. From the birth date of the eldest son, Michael, we can assume Dominick and Bridget married c. 1877. The birth certificates of the nine children could now be obtained with this information. The birth certificates will give Bridget's maiden name, and this together with a marriage date of c. 1877, deduced from the census, should guarantee the identification of the marriage certificate of Dominick and Bridget. As the Timothys were Catholic and as the townland of Ballincurry, where they lived, was served by the Catholic parish of Glinsk and Kilbegnet,

CENSUS OF IRELAND, 1901

Townland: Ballincurry   Parish: Ballinakill   Barony: Ballymoe   County: Galway

NAME AND SURNAME		RELATION to Head of Family	RELIGIOUS PROFESSION	EDUCATION	AGE	SEX	RANK PROFESSION OR OCCUPATION	MARRIAGE	WHERE BORN	IRISH LANGUAGE
Christian	Surname									
Domnick	Timothy	Head	Roman Catholic	Read write	53	M	Herd	Married	Co Galway	Irish &
Bridget	Timothy	Wife	Roman Catholic	Read write	50	F		Married	Co Galway	English
Michael	Timothy	Son	Roman Catholic	Read write	23	M	Herd	Not married	Co Galway	
James	Timothy	Son	Roman Catholic	Read write	21	M		Not married	Co Galway	
John	Timothy	Son	Roman Catholic	Read write	19	M		Not married	Co Galway	
Domnick	Timothy	Son	Roman Catholic	Read write	17	M		Not married	Co Galway	
Mary	Timothy	Daughter	Roman Catholic	Read write	15	F		Not married	Co Galway	
Denis	Timothy	Son	Roman Catholic	Read write	13	M	Scholar	Not married	Co Galway	
Bridget	Timothy	Daughter	Roman Catholic	Read write	11	F	Scholar	Not married	Co Galway	
William	Timothy	Son	Roman Catholic	Read write	9	M	Scholar	Not married	Co Galway	
Nicholas	Timothy	Son	Roman Catholic	Read write	7	M	Scholar	Not married	Co Galway	

whose registers commence in 1836, baptism entries for Dominick Timothy and his wife Bridget should be looked for. We are assuming here, of course, that Dominick and Bridget were born in or near Ballincurry. It is possible that the Timothys moved into the townland from another part of Galway sometime before 1901. The only clue the census gives to their birthplace is County Galway. It is very noticeable that in the Timothy family only the mother and father could speak Irish, the children being solely English speakers. By the turn of the 20th century, the Gaelic language was generally disappearing as children began to use English at school and home.

The 1911 census return for the Boyle family of Maas, County Donegal identifies three generations. Again with the information provided the relevant birth and marriage certificates should be easily obtainable. With the 1911 census you can be even more sure of the approximate marriage date. A family tree can be constructed to highlight the information contained in this return.

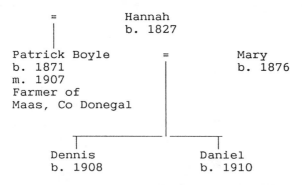

The 1901 and 1911 census returns for all Ireland are held in the National Archives, Dublin. The returns were gathered either by townland or by street, in the case of towns. This means the appropriate returns can be identified very quickly if you know the townland or street your ancestor lived in.

THE GRIFFITHS VALUATION AND TITHE APPLOTMENT BOOKS

Owing to the destruction of most early 19th century and mid-19th century census returns in Ireland, the Griffiths Valuation and Tithe Applotment Books are records of extreme importance to family researchers. These two distinct records are considered together in this section because of the combined surname indexes to them, produced by the National Library of Ireland in the 1960s. To date this index, *An Index of Surnames of Householders in Griffith's Primary Valuation and Tithe Applotment Books*, better known as the "Householders Index," is the most significant contribution to genealogical research in Ireland.

The Tithe Applotment Books were compiled by civil parishes in the period 1823 to 1837, and list all tenants who paid tithe, a tax based on the size and quality of a tenant's farm, to the Established Church of Ireland. The tithe books, naturally enough, only identify heads of rural households. They give no details on family members, as they merely list the heads of household, together with the size of the farm, and their townland address. For example, the tithe book for Killardry parish, then better known as Killaldriff parish, County Tipperary identifies Thomas Dwyer farming 20 acres and paying a tithe of L1 10d in the townland of Ballydrehid.

CENSUS OF IRELAND, 1911

Townland: Maas   Parish: Inishkeel   Barony: Boylagh   County: Donegal

NAME AND SURNAME		RELATION to Head of Family	RELIGIOUS PROFESSION	EDUCATION	AGE	RANK PROFESSION OR OCCUPATION	MARRIAGE				WHERE BORN	IRISH LANGUAGE
Christian Name	Surname							Years married	Children			
									Born Alive	Still Living		
Patrick	Boyle	Head	Roman Catholic	Read & write	40	Farmer	Married				Co Donegal	Irish &
Mary	Boyle	Wife	Roman Catholic	Read & write	35		Married	4	2	2	Co Donegal	English
Denis	Boyle	Son	Roman Catholic	Read & write	3		Single				Co Donegal	
Daniel	Boyle	Son	Roman Catholic	Read & write	1		Single				Co Donegal	
Hannagh	Boyle	Mother	Roman Catholic	Read & write	74	Retired Farmer	Widow				Co Donegal	Irish & English

As tithe books exist for most parishes in Ireland, they act as census substitutes for rural Ireland before the famine. The tithe books, in many instances, will be the last official record of many who emigrated from Ireland during the famine.

The main, if not sole, reason for using the tithe books is to identify the townland address of an ancestor. Knowledge of a townland address gives access to many other record sources. In our example, the local Catholic parish registers, namely Bansha and Kilmoyler, which date back to 1820, could be searched for Dwyer entries. The local graveyards should be visited, the Ordnance Survey sheet number 75, which maps Ballydrehid townland at six inches to one mile, should be consulted to identify them. The tithe book for Killardry parish was compiled in 1834, so the Griffiths Valuation for the same parish which was carried out in 1851 should be checked to see if the Dwyers continued to live in Ballydrehid. The Griffiths Valuation, in fact, identified four Dwyer households living in the townland: Michael farming 10 acres, James 14 acres, Jeremiah 3 acres and Julia 24 acres. This illustrates the major limitation of the tithe books and Griffiths Valuation, namely the lack of sufficient information to make family connections. We will need to rely on church registers to make the link between the Thomas Dwyer identified in 1834 and the four Dwyers living in Ballydrehid in 1851. The 1901 and 1911 census returns could also be checked for Dwyers.

The original volumes of the tithe books are held in the National Archives, Dublin and Public Record Office, Belfast. As the tithe books were hand written and compiled before standards in the spelling of both surnames and place names became estab-lished, care should be taken in researching them. For example, the townland known today as Tonaghbane in Kildrumsherdan parish, County Cavan appears as thus in the Griffiths Valuation, but was spelt in the tithe book as both Tonaghbawn and Tunnagbaun. In researching the McKay family of Drumard townland, Tamlaght O'Crilly parish, County Londonderry I noted three different spellings of the name in three different records! It was McCoy in the 1831 census, McCay in the tithe book of 1833 and McKay in the Griffiths Valuation of 1859.

The Griffiths Valuation, or Primary valuation of Ireland, was carried out under the direction of Sir Richard Griffith to determine the amount of tax each person should pay towards the support of the poor within their poor law union. The resultant survey, bound in volumes for each poor law union, was completed between 1848 and 1864. Each volume was, in turn, arranged by barony and civil parish with an index to the townlands appearing in that volume. The record is comprehensive in that it listed all property holders, no matter how insignificant the amount of land or size of house they occupied. The original volumes of the survey are now held in the National Archives, Dublin and Public Record Office, Belfast. As the records are type written, except for a few parishes in the Province of Munster, there will be no problem in interpreting surnames and place names.

As with the tithe books, the main reason for using the Griffiths Valuation is to identify the townland address of an ancestor. The actual information provided is rather limited. For example, the volume for Ennis Union, County Clare identifies Michael Kennealy renting a house, with no land attached to it, from the landlord Thomas Studdert in the townland of Bunratty East, Bunratty Parish. In addition to supplying the landlord's name, the Griffiths Valuation gives the first edition six-inch Ordnance Survey sheet number or numbers for each townland, and very importantly, a map reference number in the left hand margin.

As maps were compiled to accompany the Griffiths Valuation, an ancestor's property may be identified and then located on the ground, if it still stands.

The value of the Griffiths Valuation and Tithe Applotment Books in identifying an ancestor's homeland is further enhanced by the Householders Index which, although created one hundred years later, is now seen as an integral part of these two records. All surnames of householders appearing in both these records are indexed. The indexes are compiled on a county basis with every surname appearing in the county recorded against its constituent baronies and, most importantly, its civil parishes. For the Griffiths Valuation the index will identify the number of times the surname you are researching appears in any parish in Ireland. For the tithe books it will tell you of a surname's existence in any particular parish but not how many times the name occurs.

The index is very simple to use, you simply consult the contents page to identify the parish index you require. Even if you do not know the ancestral home, it is very feasible to systematically work your way through every parish in a county to locate where, exactly, your surname occurred. Where you go from here depends essentially on how frequently the surname appears. Generally the more unique a surname is the broader the search can be.

In researching the surname Tedder, which tradition locates on the Mayo/Galway border, the index for the two counties quickly showed no such name. In Ireland, however, you should always be on the lookout for likely spelling variations of a name. So a re-evaluation of the index identified the surname Tethers in both Griffiths Valuation and tithe book for the Parish of Shrule, County Mayo. The actual Griffiths Valuation record for the parish quickly identified a John Tethers living in the town of Shrule in 1857.

In another case, a Stephen Ronaldson, who I knew farmed at Coragh in Drumgoon Parish, County Cavan, was identified in the Griffiths Valuation as Stephen Randalson.

When I was researching the surname Eves in County Fermanagh, the index quickly showed only two parishes with that surname and within 15 minutes I was able to identify them in the Griffiths Valuation, carried out in that area in 1862. They were John Eaves at Dooraa South townland, Drumkeeran Parish and Adam Eves in the town of Kesh, Magheraculmoney Parish.

As the two examples of Tedder and Eves show, the Householders Index is indispensable to those researching uncommon names. The index, however, will be of little use to those, with no idea of the origins of their ancestor, who are researching a common name. For example, you could not justify a search of either the Griffiths Valuation or tithe books for the surname McMahon, if all you know is that they came from County Clare. The index shows that at the time of the Griffiths Valuation there were 661 McManon households in the county. The Breakdown by barony begins:

61	in	Bunratty Lower	43	Inchiquin
19		Bunratty Upper	86	Islands
25		Burren	90	Moyarta
112		Clonderalaw	33	Tulla Lower
57		Corcomroe	55	Tulla Upper
80		Ibrickan		

On the other hand, if you knew your McMahon ancestry came from Abbey Parish in the barony of Burren, then a search of the Griffiths Valuation would be very worthwhile. The index shows five McMahon households in this parish in 1855.

With the seven record sources detailed in this chapter, you should be able to construct a family tree on most family lines going back six or seven generations. Each of the records will supply a wealth of relevant information on their own account. But equally important, each of these sources and the information they contain, hold clues to aid the identification of other sources. By this process of one line of research leading to another, a family tree will spring to life.

Don't despair if you find the church register you require was destroyed or starts too late. Obstacles are there to be surmounted, if one avenue shuts its doors to you, look for another. You might identify a gravestone listing three generations of your ancestors. Initially, you might be disappointed that your ancestor was born in 1863, thus missing out on civil registration, but their later identification in a baptism register will more than compensate for it. In fact, there is nothing quite like the excitement of identifying an ancestor you, at one time, thought was lost to you.

OTHER RECORD SOURCES

The seven record sources described in the previous chapter will be the starting points for those researching their family tree. The sources described in this section are very valuable to the family researcher, but I would advise turning to them only after exhausting the seven major sources. The major records, in all cases, will be more comprehensive in terms of family detail provided and in terms of their coverage of Ireland.

The early census returns of 1821, 1831, 1841 and 1851 would be classified as major record sources if they had survived for much greater areas of Ireland. Census substitutes, such as the hearth money rolls of the 1660s and the Flax Growers' Lists of 1796, don't list all heads of household. Although records in the Registry of Deeds date back to 1708, there is no guarantee an ancestor would have registered his property transactions. Records of great genealogical value may be found, but again there is no certainty, among the business records of the large-landed estates.

NEWSPAPERS

Birth notices, marriage announcements, and obituaries contained within the pages of newspapers can provide very useful information, especially when it is remembered that many towns in Ireland had their own paper. In Dublin by the mid-1750s *Faulkner's Dublin Journal*, the *Freeman's Journal*, the *Dublin Hibernian Journal* and *Dublin Evening Post* were beginning to carry regular and fairly numerous marriage and obituary notices for the city and county of Dublin. Many provincial towns also had newspapers dating back to the 18th century, such as the *Belfast Newsletter* from 1737, *Cork Journal* from 1753, *Limerick Chronicle* from 1768 and the *Londonderry Journal* from 1772.

The problem with newspapers, and searching through them, is that because of the frequency of their publication, it is very crucial to be able to narrow down the field of search to a fairly precise date. The time spent looking up newspapers, however, is well justified, especially if it comes up with an obituary, as they can provide a quite detailed life history. For example:

OBITUARY of Samuel Patton Mitchell

"The Rev. S.P. Mitchell, Rector of St. Nicholas, Belfast. Graduate of Trinity College, Dublin Ordained deacon for the diocese of Kilmore in 1895, afterwards being curate of Drumgoon, County Cavan. The following year he was appointed curate of Seapatrick, Banbridge where he remained until 1900, when he came to St. Thomas' Belfast. He took over the supervision of the new district of St. Nicholas' and in 1901 became its first rector. He was largely responsible for the erection of the fine church on Lisburn Road which will always be regarded as a memorial to him."

DIRECTORIES

These are a useful source of information for people living in the towns of Ireland. The directories were usually organized by trade, such as grocers, bankers, publicans, coopers, ship builders, tanners, rope makers and brewers, to name but a few. Under each trade were listed the people carrying out that trade, together with their address. The local gentry, clergy, and professional people were also noted.

The first trade directory for Dublin city appeared in 1751, and by 1799, the list of merchants within its pages exceeded 4,300. The first provincial town to issue a directory was Limerick in 1769, to be followed by Cork in 1787. In 1820, J. Pigot & Co. issued the *Commercial Directory of Ireland*, covering the main towns. Further editions appeared in 1824, 1846, 1856, 1870, 1881 and 1894. The National Archives, Dublin and the Public Record Office, Belfast and the National Library of Ireland hold the greatest number of directories, but the local libraries will hold directories for their local area.

SCHOOL REGISTERS

The widespread and comprehensive keeping of school registers had to await the introduction of the national system of schooling in 1832 and, in particular, the 1860s, when many registers start. Prior to 1832, schooling depended on support from churches, charitable endowments and private funding. The second report of the Commissioners of Irish Education Inquiry of 1826-7 does list all schools, on a parish basis, together with the number and religion of their pupils. It furthermore names all teachers. Few registers, however, survive for these schools.

The national schoolhouse became a feature of the Irish countryside in the second half of the 19th century and the school registers they kept can be of great value to the genealogist. To identify the appropriate register, you need to know at least the parish your ancestor lived in, as in the nine counties of Ulster alone 2,500 national schools were established between 1832 and 1860. The information provided of name, date of birth and religion of pupil, together with the father's occupation and address, should be sufficient to enable the identification of an ancestor, even in those areas where your surname is common. The National Archives, Dublin and the Public Record Office, Belfast hold many school registers.

HEARTH MONEY ROLLS

The first Hearth Money act was passed in the Irish parliament in 1662 as a means to increase government revenue. A tax of two shillings was to be raised for every hearth or "other place used for firing." A list was then kept by county, giving the name and amount each householder had to pay under their townland. Copies of the hearth lists subsequently drawn up between 1663 and 1666 exist in full for the Ulster counties of Antrim, Armagh, Donegal, Fermanagh, Londonderry, Monaghan, and Tyrone and for Counties Dublin, Kilkenny, Louth, Sligo, Tipperary, Westmeath and Wicklow. Extracts, however, do survive for other counties.

FLAX GROWERS' LISTS

In 1796, a list was compiled by parish of farmers who were entitled to a grant for sowing flax seed. The grant was to be in the form of equipment used in the linen industry, i.e. weaving looms or, more usually, spinning wheels. The province of Ulster was, by this time, a centre of the linen industry and most farmers would have had some proportion of their land under flax. To be entitled to one spinning wheel, a farmer had to have just one rood, i.e. one quarter of one acre, of land planted with "good sound flax seeds." Every county in Ireland had such lists drawn up. They can be consulted in the Linen Hall Library, Belfast.

THE RELIGIOUS CENSUS OF 1766

In 1766, the Church of Ireland clergy were instructed to draw up a return of householders in their parishes and show their religion. An example of the returns show great variations in their usefulness. For example, the return for Cumber parish, County Londonderry merely gives a numerical breakdown of Protestants and Catholics in each of its constituent townlands. It, therefore, serves no purpose for the genealogist. The return for Nantinan Parish, County Limerick names all Protestant householders but doesn't provide their townland address, while that for Artrea Parish, County Tyrone lists against each townland the occupiers and their religion.

Unfortunately, none of the 1766 returns list all members of a household. This makes for problems of identification in areas where the same surname occurs frequently.

EARLY 19th CENTURY CENSUS RECORDS

The government carried out census enumerations for all Ireland in 1821, 1831, 1841 and 1851, but, unfortunately, the returns don't survive for many areas.

The example of one such return from the 1821 census for Inisheer Island, County Galway, shows what a serious loss this is to the genealogist.

With this return it is possible to calculate the approximate dates of birth for all members of the family and deduce the marriage date of the parents. It can be assumed that Pat Faherty married Bridget around 1811, as their first born son was aged 9 in 1821. (Never, though, rely on alleged ages of adults as being accurate, use them only as a guide!) The observation column provides very interesting information as to how the occupants of one of the Arran Islands earned their living.

The National Archives, Dublin hold these surviving census records. The loss of census returns for many areas has meant that records such as the tithe books and Griffith's Valuation, which survive for all Ireland, have taken on an added importance.

PLANTATION AND SETTLEMENT RECORDS

Various 17th century surveys record the changes in ownership and occupation resulting from the land confiscations of that period. The extensive changes in landownership following the Cromwellian settlement are recorded in the Civil Survey and Down Survey, both begun in 1654. Confiscated lands were identified, surveyed and mapped to record land ownership, land boundaries, and land use, whether wood, bog, mountain, arable, meadow or pasture. In all, 27 counties were surveyed in the Civil Survey, while all counties except Galway, Roscommon and Mayo were mapped in the Down Survey.

The Books of Survey and Distribution followed, owing to the need to establish land ownership following the restoration of Charles II in 1660 and further forfeitures resulting from an Act of 1688. The Books of Survey and Distribution, as the example from County Clare shows, can show up to three different landowners for any given area through the 17th century.

CENSUS OF IRELAND, 1821

Townland: Inisheer   Parish: Arran   Barony: Arran   County: Galway

No of House	No of Stories	NAMES OF INHABITANTS	AGE	OCCUPATION	No of Acres	OBSERVATIONS
1	1	Pat Faherty	40	Farmer & Fisherman	Cartron $\frac{1}{4}$	The inhabitants of this Island live by fishing and kelp making they take large quantities of Cod Ling Haddock Glassin and Herrings from Christmas to the Middle of April when they commence kelp making which they continue to the end of September the best kelp at the Galway Market is here manufactured
		Bridget Faherty his wife	30			The land here and in all the Islands of Arran is never in any instance let by the acre it is set by the parcell Denominated Quarters Half Quarters Cartrons Half Cartrons fourths of Cartrons Eights of Cartrons and Sixteenths of Cartrons
		Margaret Faherty Daughter	9			The Tillage is mostly potatoes with very little Rye in this Island.
		John Faherty Son	6			
		Peter Faherty Son	3			
		Kate Faherty Daughter	1			
		Ned Tolan	18	House Servant		
		Anthony Joyce	35	A Schoolmaster unemployed		

Parish: Digart   Barony: Inchiquin   County: Clare

Col 1	2	3	4	5	6	7	8	9
101	Teige O'Bryan	Carrowmenough Arable & Pasture	73	73	Lord Clare	73	Francis Burton	⊕

EXPLANATION OF THE BOOKS OF SURVEY AND DISTRIBUTION

Col. 1   Reference number in the Down Survey Parish map.
Col. 2   Proprietor in 1640/1641.
Col. 3   Name of townland and description of the land.
Col. 4   Number of acres of cultivable land.
Col. 5   Number of acres redistributed after the Cromwellian settlement.
Col. 6   Name of proprietor established by Charles II.
Col. 7   Number of acres purchased after the forfeiture of 1688.
Col. 8   Name of the purchaser of the land forfeited after 1688. If column 8 is blank, it indicates that the landowner who acquired the land under Charles II continued to retain it in 1703.
Col. 9   The ⊕ symbol after the purchaser's name in Column 8 indicates that he was a purchaser of a forfeited estate of 1688, at the Trustee's sale, 1701-1703.

THE REGISTRY OF DEEDS

The registry of Deeds is undoubtedly a very useful source, as it holds a variety of records relating to property transactions dating back to 1708. Two factors are perhaps responsible for this source not being as extensively used as it might be.

Although the most common transaction registered was the lease, and most farms in Ireland were held by lease, there is no guarantee that an ancestor's lease or property transaction was registered. As deeds were only registered when the interested parties elected to do so, there is no means of predicting the existence of a deed. As a general rule, small farmers and cottiers rarely figure in registered deeds, whereas merchants, traders and substantial farmers were more likely to figure in deeds.

The indexes to the Deeds are quite complicated to use and they can easily deter a first-time user. The name indexes are arranged in volumes, consisting of a number of years, in alphabetical order by name of the grantor, i.e. the landlord. Against the name of the grantor is given the grantee's name and, after 1833 but not before, their address. A volume, page and deed number will then direct you to the actual register:

INDEX TO GRANTORS

Volume D, 1768 to 1776

GRANTOR		GRANTEE	REFERENCE TO REGISTER		
Surname	Christian Name	Surname	Volume	Page	Deed Number
Darling	Robert	Gould	279	325	182991

To use the name indexes, you need to know the landlord of your ancestor. The immediate lessor column in the Griffith's Valuation will identify the mid-19th century landlords. It is possible, of course, that a tenant or grantee became a grantor if he, for example, sublet part of his holdings. In this case your ancestor will appear in alphabetical order in the name index.

The land indexes are arranged in volumes, by county or city, for a period of years, in alphabetical order under the initial letter of the townland or street. If you know, therefore, the townland or street in which your ancestor lived, then it may be possible to trace transactions associated with the family back through time:

LAND INDEX, 1821 to 1825.   COUNTY OF WEXFORD

Townland	Parties Names: Grantors to Grantees	Reference:		
		Vol.	Page	Deed no:
Chappel	Boyd & others to Redmond	771	271	522806
Churchtown	Boyd & another to Redmond & another	771	272	522807

The land index provides the surname of both the principal grantor and grantee. In the above example, Boyd will be indexed in the name indexes, as he is a grantor, but Redmond will not be.

The above indexes refer to the sworn copy, or "memorial," of the deed presented at the Registry of Deeds in Dublin, and not to the actual deed, which after registration is returned to the solicitor or his agent. On registration, the memorial was retained, given a reference number and indexed in the Names Index and, prior to 1947, in the Lands Index. The memorial provides the fullest statement of the contents of a deed that the Registry holds.

A rewarding search of the Registry of Deeds will probably be time consuming and require a lot of care. The Registry, therefore, should probably be left alone until at least estate records have been examined.

ESTATE RECORDS

The pattern of great family estates established with the confiscations, plantations and settlements in the period to 1703 remained largely unchanged until they were finally broken up in the latter years of the 19th century under the Land Acts. Most of the acreage of Ireland was held in large estates. In 1871, 19 estates varied in size from 50,000 to 160,000 acres, 254 were in the range of 10,000 to 50,000 acres, while 418 were of 5,000 to 10,000 acres. These estates, because of their size, were run on a business basis in which records had to be kept of tenants' leases, rent payments and other such matters. Three records in particular are of great genealogical value, namely leases, rent receipt books and surveys. I will deal with each in turn.

LEASES

Most Irish land was held by lease and, until the end of the

18th century, the most common form of lease seems to have been that for three lives. A lease for lives meant that the tenant qualified as a freeholder and was thus entitled to vote, which tended to strengthen the political "interest" of the landlord. The lives mentioned in the lease, of course, provide a great deal of useful genealogy. On the death of the longest living of the three stipulated lives, the lease would expire. The lease below, commencing on the 1st November 1779, for William Patton's farm in Carrickanany, County Armagh, didn't expire until the death of John Patton on the 3rd of May 1857.

"This indenture made 28 September 1781 between the Right Honourable Lord Gosford and William Patton of the townland of Carrickanany in the County of Armagh.

In consideration of the yearly rent, duties, covenants and agreements herein Lord Gosford doth demise, grant, set and to farm let unto the said William Patton and his heirs all the farm of land in the townland of Carrickanany now in the actual possession of William Patton containing by estimate 43 acres 3 roods 10 perches English statute measure together with 1 acre 20 perches of turf bog only granted for firing for the use of the premises. All which concern are situate in the parish of Loughgilly barony of Fews and County of Armagh. Lord Gosford reserves a full liberty of opening a road through said farm should he think it necessary.

To hold for and during the life of Robert Patton now about 16 years old, also for and during the life of John Patton now about 14 years old, also for and during the life of George Patton now about 11 years old (3 sons of the lessee William Patton) or for and during the life of the longest lives of them commencing from 1 November 1779.

The said William Patton paying every year the rent of L18 11s 1d, together with 12 pence per pound receivers fee, together with the carriage of 4 barrels of coal to be brought in good sound sacks either from Newry or Tyrone Coal pits as Lord Gosford shall please to appoint. And in case of refusal to go when called upon or not delivering the full measure at the mansion house at Gosford Castle to forfeit 4s 4d in lieu of each barrel of coals not delivered.

And the said William Patton covenants for himself and his heirs that within 3 years from the date hereof he will enclose at least 1 acre of said premises for an orchard . . . and there plant apple trees in lines 31 feet by 21 feet asunder (The apple trees to be furnished by Lord Gosford with William Patton to pay Lord Gosford's gardener one halfpenny for each apple tree) . . .

William Patton, his heirs and their under tenants shall grind all their corn, malt, grain at one of the manor mills belonging to Lord Gosford and shall pay the toll thereof.

Obliged to ditch said farm as far as his Mearings Run with a sufficient ditch 6 feet wide and 5 feet deep and also to divide his farm into convenient fields with ditches 4 feet by 5 feet and to set in the face of all the ditches so made one row of white thorn or Crab tree quicks at the distance of 4 inches one quick from the other. And also to plant the face of such ditches so made with Oak, Ash or Elm at the distance of 21 feet asunder.

Signed and sealed by Lord Gosford and William Patton."

The following family tree can be deduced from the above lease:

William Patton, farmer of Carrickanany

| Robert
b. 1765 | John
b. 1767 | George
b. 1770 |

In addition to this genealogical information, a lease provides interesting information on the conditions attached to the granting of it. For example, Lord Gosford expected William Patton to enclose his farm, plant an orchard, use the manor mill and carry coal to Gosford castle.

RENT RECEIPT BOOKS

When rent receipt books, kept by the landlord or his agent, extend over a lengthy period of time, it is often possible to follow changes in farm occupation. For example, the rent receipt book for Lord Gosford's Armagh estate shows that sometime between November 1822 and May 1823, Robert Patton died as his wife began to pay the rent:

Rent Receiving Book--Armagh Estate

Name	Robert Patton	Widow Patton
Townland	Carrickanany	Carrickanany
Account No.	416	416
Rent	L9 14s 9 1/2d	L9 14s 9 1/2d
For half year to	November 1822	May 1823

SURVEYS

Landlords quite frequently commissioned surveys of their estates which were often accompanied by maps identifying tenants' holdings.

In 1821, William Greig submitted a report to Lord Gosford on the state of his 8,000-acre estate in County Armagh. Greig collected information on every holding on the estate and mapped them. The value of such a survey can be gauged by the fact that 3,000 people lived within the area so surveyed.

Greig's map of William Patton's lease, described previously, is produced below and shows that William Patton's original lease of 43 acres in 1779 was, by 1820, subdivided into seven farms. The map, furthermore, names the farmers.

The survey provides the following description against the above lease: "Farm No. 10 William Patton senior--now held by his sons Robert, George, and John and their sub tenants. Scarce any improvement seems to have been made on this farm.
John Patton resides in Carrowmannon.
George is only resident sometimes.
Robert occupies the corn mill and has lately built a good flax mill but he and his family seem most slovenly.

This farm at the expiration of the lease might be let in 3 divisions. Only 2 divisions would be profitable. George doesn't deserve any part the buildings on his part are in the most ruinous condition and he seldom occupies much of the land himself.

46

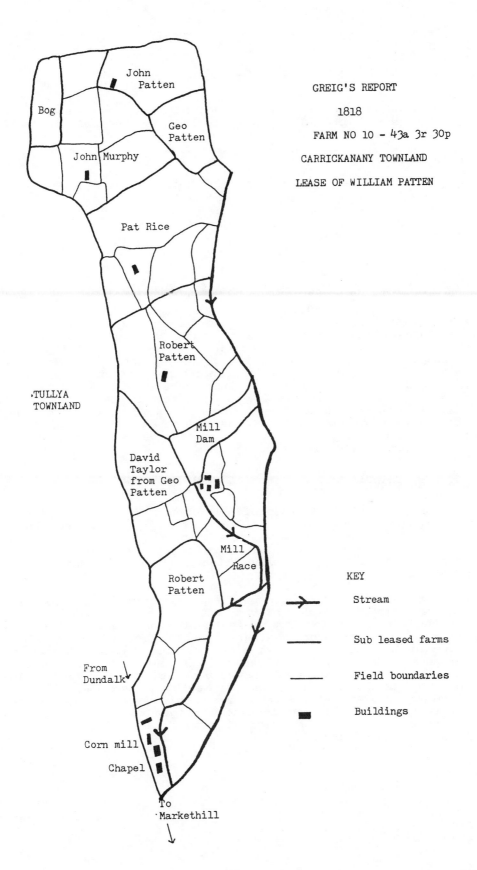

GREIG'S REPORT

1818

FARM NO 10 - 43a 3r 30p

CARRICKANANY TOWNLAND

LEASE OF WILLIAM PATTEN

John
Patten

Bog

Geo
Patten

John Murphy

Pat Rice

Robert
Patten

‚TULLYA
TOWNLAND

Mill
Dam

David
Taylor
from Geo
Patten

Mill
Race

Robert
Patten

From
Dundalk

Corn mill

Chapel

To
·Markethill

KEY

⟶ Stream

—— Sub leased farms

— Field boundaries

▬ Buildings

47

arable	42a	1r	10p
chapel yard & mill dam	1	2	20
Total	43	3	30

In addition to this background material about each leased farm, the survey provides quite detailed genealogical information on each family on the estate:

CARROWMANNON

Family	John Patton age 45. Wife age 40
	4 children -- 3 boys age 10 to 17
	1 girl age 5
Servants	1 man
	1 maid
	1 cottier
Religion	Protestant
Character	Rather slovenly but opulent

It is clear that the amount of information, both genealogical and historical, that can be gleaned from surveys such as Greig's are immense. Greig highlighted two problems on the Gosford estate that give some idea of conditions existing in 19th century Ireland. One was the high level of rents, based on a prosperous domestic linen industry rather than on the productive capacity of the land, and the other was the substantial subdivision of holdings. John Patton's 25 acres lease in Carrowmannon, for example, was sublet to five farmers who were also linen weavers with nine looms among them. The report states that these sub-tenants were "very industrious but excessive rents made them very poor and in great arrears to Patton."

ORDNANCE SURVEY MEMOIRS

As a prelude to a nationwide valuation of land and buildings, the Ordnance Survey was, in 1824, directed to map the whole of Ireland. The resultant maps, at six inches to one mile, appeared between 1835 and 1846. In the Griffith's Valuation, every townland in Ireland was identified against an Ordnance Survey sheet number.

It was intended to accompany the maps with written topographical descriptions which, however, were never published except that for the parish of Templemore in County Londonderry. The Field Officers did, however, gather much historical, geographical, economic and social information for many parishes in their notebooks, which have survived to this day. In addition to the nine counties of Ulster, memoirs exist for counties Galway, Leitrim, Leix, Longford, Mayo, Meath, Roscommon, Sligo and Tipperary. These memoirs can provide useful genealogical information, as in many instances emigrants, farmers and mill owners are named. The original memoirs are held in the Royal Irish Academy in Dublin.

IRISH GENEALOGY AND THE INTERNET

The internet has been described as "the modern way to trace your family tree". The internet is in reality one vast network of computers that electronically connects millions of people worldwide, and in so doing allows people and organisations, scattered all over the world, to share their knowledge and experiences.

The world wide web is the most popular method of presenting information on the internet. This information can be presented in multimedia formats such as text, graphics, sound, animation and video. The web is, in effect, an electronic library that covers the entire globe and each location or web site accessible on the internet represents a book. Each web site has a contents page which guides access to other pages on the web site, as well as to other web sites.

The internet is ideally suited for people researching their ancestors, whether they are beginners or experienced researchers, as the range of material accessible on the internet is simply quite breathtaking. Indeed the world wide web is quite painless to navigate once you have used it for the first time. As information contained on the world wide web consists of links (represented by underlined words and accessed by clicking your mouse on them) from one page to another and from one web site to another web site it quite often means that once you have established a line of inquiry it leads naturally to further information of interest.

For those who still feel more comfortable with the written word two books by Cyndi Howells (both published by the Genealogical Publishing Company) provide an extensive introduction to using the internet for research purposes. The titles of these books are *Netting Your Ancestors: Genealogical Research on the Internet* and *Cyndi's List: The Book: A comprehensive list of 40,000 genealogy sites on the Internet.*

In *Netting Your Ancestors* Cyndi Howells, the creator and webmaster of Cyndi's List of Genealogy Sites on the Internet, demonstrates how to take maximum advantage of the internet in genealogical research. This book focuses on the three most useful components of the Internet: E-mail, Mailing Lists and Newsgroups, and the World Wide Web.

The quickest and most direct way to access information on the world wide web is knowledge of the web site addresses of where the information you require is held. For newcomers to the internet researching their Irish ancestry I would recommend visiting the following three sites:

- www.genuki.org.uk/big/irl
- www.cyndislist.com
- www.ireland.com/ancestor

The www.genuki.org.uk/big/irl web site provides detailed information on the genealogy scene in Ireland by the means of either selecting the county of interest to the researcher or by selecting a topic of interest to the user under the INFORMATION RELATED TO ALL OF IRELAND heading. The topics in the latter section include:

Archives and Libraries	Heraldry
Bibliography	History
Biography	Land and Property
Cemeteries	Maps
Census	Military History
Chronology	Names, Geographical
Church Records	Names, Personal
Civil Registration	Newspapers
Court Records	Nobility
Description and Travel	Occupations
Directories	Periodicals
Emigration and Immigration	Probate Records
Gazetteers	Social Life and Customs
Genealogy	Societies
	Taxation

Thus, if you are attempting to find out information about record offices in Ireland a useful starting point might be to click (with the mouse on your computer) on the Archives and Libraries link which in turn offers access to information under links such as Local libraries in Northern Ireland, Local libraries in the Republic of Ireland, and Major repositories.

If you wanted to access online Irish newspapers such as the *Irish Times*, the *Irish News*, the *Irish Independent* or the *Examiner* all you need to do is access the Newspapers link.

I would also highly recommend an examination of Cyndi's List of Genealogy Sites on the Internet at www.cyndislist.com. This site, compiled by Cyndi Howells, is accessed by an extensive category index which is listed in alphabetical order. By clicking on Ireland and Northern Ireland you enter a library dedicated to genealogical issues in Ireland. This library of information is, in turn, accessed by the following Category Index headings:

General Resource Sites
GENUKI Resources by County
Government & Cities
History & Culture
How To
Irish Family History Foundation - County Heritage Centres
Libraries, Archives & Museums

By clicking on General Resource Sites you could find out further information about Irish genealogy websites by clicking on The A to Z of Irish Genealogy Web Sites link.

Links to each of Ireland's network of genealogy centres, usually established on a county basis, can be accessed by clicking on the category index heading Irish Family History Foundation - County Heritage Centres.

The beginner tracing their Irish roots might wish to access the Finding Your Ancestors in Ireland link in the How To category index.

If you needed to identify professional genealogists in Ireland a useful starting point would be the Professional Researchers, Volunteers & Other Research Services link. This site, at present, has links to 20 other sites offering either research services or lists of genealogists who can be commissioned to conduct research through Irish record sources. Sites such as Association of Professional Genealogists in Ireland or The National Archives of Ireland: Genealogical and Historical Researchers can be directly accessed from this link.

These few examples demonstrate that nearly any question forming in your mind about tracing Irish roots can be answered somewhere on the world wide web.

In the Records: Census, Cemeteries, Land, Obituaries, Personal, Taxes and Vital category of Cyndi's List there are even searchable databases such as Irish Famine Migration To New Brunswick, 1845-1852 and Leitrim-Roscommon 1901 Census Home Page.

The WorldGenWeb project, which is hosted by Rootsweb.com, is a non-commerical, volunteer based organisation which is committed to "Connecting the world through genealogy". Their aim is to set up every country in the world with its own GenWeb site which links to regional genealogy sources. By clicking on WorldGenWeb

<u>Project</u> in Cyndi's List you gain access to the Ireland GenWeb projects by clicking on a county of interest.

By clicking on <u>Kilkenny</u>, for example, you gain access to County Kilkenny Genealogy and History which is hosted on <u>www.rootsweb.com/~irlkik</u>. This site includes maps of the parishes and towns of County Kilkenny together with detailed listings of available record sources for the county. There is also an alphabetical listing of the townlands in the county.

The **Irish Ancestors** web site at <u>www.ireland.com/ancestor</u> site, published by the Irish Times and maintained by John Grenham (author of the very comprehensive *Tracing your Irish Ancestors*, published by Gill & Macmillan, Dublin), is another "must visit" site for people interested in tracing their Irish roots.

Access to this extensive reference library for Irish genealogy is through 5 topics, namely:

What's in a name? - What do you know about your surname?
Placenames - Identify your place of origin
Magazine - Emigration, heraldry, the origin of surnames...
Gen.ie - A complete personalised guide to the records relevant to your Irish ancestor
Browse - Wander through the records for yourself ..or check out our links

By clicking on the <u>What's in a name</u> icon you can search their database for historical information about your ancestor's surname. If a search is successful it will provide information on the distribution and variant spellings of the surname together with details of published family histories. It also offers the opportunity to purchase details of how your surname came into being together with a Coat of Arms where relevant.

As "the single most important item of information for Irish family history research is a precise place of origin" the Irish Ancestor site, by clicking on <u>Placenames</u>, provides visitors with the opportunity to search the entire Townland Index of Ireland, together with street listings from Dublin, Cork and Belfast cities. For example a placename search of this database for the placename Ballycastle reveals that there are two towns in Ireland called Ballycastle, one in County Antrim and the other in Mayo, and three townlands of the name in Counties Antrim, Derry and Down. The search results also identify the civil parish and poor law union address for each relevant entry found.

If you would like a personalised guide to the records - their dates, locations, reference numbers, publication information - that might be relevant for you in researching a particular Irish ancestor then you might wish to complete the form provided at the <u>Gen.ie</u> link. It must be stressed that this service does not include searches of the actual record sources.

In the Browse section of the Irish Ancestors' site you gain access to much useful information through the six category headings of the records, counties, emigration, addresses, how to and links. For example the records link provides detailed information on each of the major genealogical records in Ireland. The How to link provides some strategies for dealing with some of the more common research scenarios such as your ancestor was not born and did not marry or die in Ireland after 1863 and you don't know where in Ireland he or she came from.

Indeed there is so much information on these web sites that no matter how many times you come back to them you can always find something of interest. For example the Links site of Irish Ancestors provides access to many passenger lists. In picking one at random, namely the ship Creole which sailed from Londonderry for Philadelphia in 1834, it directed me to the **Immigrant Ships Transcribers Guild** (hosted on http://istg.rootsweb.com). Not only does this site record the names of passengers who sailed on the Creole but it gives a very informative history of the ship. Of particular interest to me was the fact that this ship normally traded out of the port of Derry under the flag of McCorkell & Co. McCorkell & Co, established in 1778, was one of the big Derry-owned shipping companies of the 19th century. And in the year 2000 a direct descendant of this family, namely John McCorkell, set up a dotcom business at www.mccorkellline.com to sell memorabilia depicting the ships which carried tens of thousands of Irish emigrants to the Americas. This attractive web site displays pictures and histories of many of the McCorkell passenger ships, including their flagship the *Minnehaha*, which was known in New York as the "Green Yacht from Derry".

There are a growing number of searchable databases on the internet. For example on Rootsweb, at www.rootsweb.com, which claims to be "the oldest and largest free genealogy site" you can search over 40 major databases at RootsWeb in one search and over 650 million names recorded in Ancestry.com by simply entering the last name and first name of an ancestor. In addition there are many links on Rootsweb to keep an avid web explorer happy for a very long time!

A project such as FreeBMD, which stands for Free Births, Marriages and Deaths, hosted at http://freebmd.rootsweb.com shows the potential, and idealism, of voluntary effort in building up online databases. FreeBMD project's objective is to provide free internet access to the Civil Registration index information for England and Wales. Free BMD's database currently stands at over 2 million records.

Scots Origins, on behalf of the General Register Office for Scotland, at www.origins.net/gro provides exclusive internet access, on a pay per view basis, to the official genealogical information for Scotland. Amounting to 25 million names this database consists of the old parish registers dating from 1553 to 1854, civil birth, marriage and death registers from 1855 to 1900 and the censuses of 1881 and 1891.

These examples clearly demonstrate the scale and power of online databases. It is unfortunate that online databases of this scale have not been compiled for Irish record sources. The database of the Church of Jesus Christ of Latter Day Saints is the most significant online database of Irish sources at present. The Ancestor Search facility on their site, www.familysearch.org, allows searches of "Ancestral File, International Genealogical Index, Pedigree Resource File, and Web sites" for named ancestors throughout the world, including Ireland.

The Ancestral File consists of over 35 million names organised into families and pedigrees while the International Genealogical Index comprises over 600 million names extracted from birth, marriage and death records from throughout the world. This massive database also includes family history records submitted by individuals together with thousands of web sites categorised by volunteers.

A search of this database is simple to carry out. You fill in the onscreen form with the information you hold on a particular ancestor and then click the Search button. The form consists of 12 fields:

First Name; Last Name; First Name of Father; Last Name of Father; First Name of Mother; Last Name of Mother; First Name of Spouse; Last Name of Spouse;
Event (select from a number of options eg Birth);
Year Range (select from a number of options eg + or - 10 years); Year;
Country (select from a list of countries eg Ireland)

To produce a manageable number of matches in any search (especially in a database of over 600 million entries) it makes sense to provide as much detail in the form as you can (ie fill in as many fields as you can). If you don't narrow your search down the results page will provide far too many entries from which to make rational choices. For example a search based on the last name O'Sullivan and the country Ireland returns no fewer than 1596 matches (presented in alphabetical order by first name) in the International Genealogical Index alone. I would suggest, therefore, that it is highly unlikely that you will identify your Irish ancestry if you conduct a search based on last name and country!

It makes sense to make your search more specific. The following example of an Ancestor Search produced 2 matches. I requested a search for the birth of a Jane Ann Campbell to a father Henry Campbell and mother Mary Ann in Ireland. The database identified the birth of Jane Anne Campbell on 14 March 1841 in Drumgoon, County Cavan and the christening of Jane Anne Campbell on 7 April 1841 at Ashfield, County Cavan. Both these matches were retrieved from the International Genealogical Index.

By clicking on these search results you then gain access to the full details from the International Genealogical Index which also includes source information. With this source information you can then go and verify the information. In this case a search of the baptismal registers of Ashfield Church of Ireland church confirms that Jane Anne

Campbell was born on 14 March 1841 and baptised on 7 April 1841 to parents Henry Campbell, a farmer and his wife Mary Anne in the townland of Tonaghbane, County Cavan.

To search the database for the marriage of Henry Campbell to Mary Ann between 1821 and 1841 you would select the marriage option in the Event field; the Year Range option of + or - 10 years; enter 1831 in the Year field; and select the country Ireland. This search produced 6 matches (from a potential 600 million!) in the International Genealogical Index.

You should always remember that the non-appearance of your ancestor in such a database could mean a number of things. It could be that the record detailing your ancestor has not been indexed or that the source doesn't go back far enough to record the event you are looking for or even that an error or omission was made in transcription. So be cautious in any conclusions you draw when searching databases.

As the records of the General Register Office (GRO) in Dublin for the period 1864 to 1898 are currently being digitised it does mean that in the long run the day might come (as it already has in the Scottish GRO at www.origins.net) when a dataset of civil birth, marriage and death registers for Ireland could be placed on a web site on a pay per view basis.

A number of very significant databases, however, for those people with Irish ancestry have been published in recent years on CD-ROM. The **Family Archive** CD collection, produced in association between Broderbund Software and the Genealogical Publishing Company, has added a new dimension to Irish genealogical research (www.familytreemaker.com). For example *An Index to Griffith's Valuation*, one of the major genealogical sources in Ireland, detailing some 1.25 million people can now be accessed quickly on CD-ROM in the comfort of one's home or local library. This index gives the full name of each and every householder and their county, parish and townland of residence. The value of such a source is self-evident as the Griffith's Valuation recorded all heads of household in mid-19th century Ireland. This CD-ROM relegates to a great extent the value of the Householders Index to genealogists (see chapter on Major Record Sources - The Griffith's Valuation and Tithe Books).

Other important Irish sources indexed recently on CD-ROM in the Family Archives series include indexes to: 200,000 landholders recorded in the early 19th century Tithe Books for Counties Antrim, Armagh, Derry, Down, Fermanagh and Tyrone; 60,000 heads of household recorded in the Flax Growers Lists for all Ireland; and 60,000 Irish Immigrants to North America, 1803-1871.

Eneclann (www.eneclann.ie) intends to publish a series of sources for Irish history and genealogy on CD-ROM. The first volume in this series, an *Index of Irish Wills*

1484-1858, records over 100,000 names from testamentary records in the National Archives of Ireland.

The world wide web is also a good place to identify information recorded in a more traditional form, namely books. For example a team based at the Institute of Irish Studies at Queen's University of Belfast has now transcribed, indexed and published the complete set of the Ordnance Survey memoirs, which were originally compiled in the 1830s, in 40 volumes. These 40 volumes "act as a nineteenth century Domesday book and are essential to the understanding of the cultural heritage of our communities". By examining the Institute's web site at www.qub.ac.uk/iis/publications/OrdnanceSurveyMemoirs it is quite straightforward to identify the volume which will give much insight into the parish your ancestor lived in.

Another significant and recent feature of the genealogy scene in Ireland is the fact that most of the major repositories of record sources have compiled informative web sites. The web addresses of these institutions are provided in the Glossary listing the major record offices.

The web site of the Public Record Office of Northern Ireland (http://proni.nics.gov.uk), for example, has produced some very useful online indexes such as Geographical Index, Prominent Persons Index and Presbyterian Church Index. In attempting to locate your ancestral homeland the Geographical Index can help you locate your county, parish or townland and provide an ordnance survey map reference number.

If you are interested in identifying professional genealogists to conduct research on your behalf then you will be interested in the contact details provided on the sites of both the National Library of Ireland (www.nli.ie) and the National Archives (www.nationalarchives.ie)

Details of Ireland's network of genealogy centres (which are recorded in the Glossary of Irish Genealogy Centres) can be found on the web site of the Irish Family History Foundation at www.irishroots.net.

In addition to examining web sites of specific institutions (such as the National Archives) or of compiled sites of genealogical information and links (such as cyndislist or genuki) you can also use a Search Engine such as AltaVista, Yahoo or Lycos to narrow research to a specific topic of interest to you. The search engine will then return a list of matches which are in effect links to other web sites.

For example the search engine www.lycos.com returned a list of 675 web sites in UK and Ireland when a search with the keywords "irish roots" was requested. The first match recorded was that of Irish Roots Magazine Homepage. This means that if you wish to find out more about this magazine you simply click on its underlined link.

By selecting search result number 4, <u>Irish Family History Foundation for Irish Roots,</u> the visitor will gain access to details of the county network of genealogy centres in Ireland. If you wish to gain access to a message board for family history enquiries on County Derry then you should click on web site 7, <u>Derry (Londonderry) Ireland - Bulletin Boards - Irish roots</u>.

In addition to the huge digitised library of the world wide web another useful function of the internet in helping to trace your family tree is e-mail. This electronic messaging service enables you to communicate quickly and conveniently with people all over the world. Queries to fellow researchers on the other side of the globe can be sent and replied to in a matter of hours.

Many family history societies and genealogical groups have discussion groups on the internet which can be a great source of help. Members join to share information and advice about ancestors they may be tracing.

The Usenet genealogy newsgroup is of interest to genealogists tracing their Irish roots. It is read by family historians worldwide, at <u>news:soc.genealogy.ireland,</u> to ask others about family names and to exchange information on what to read or where to go.

To sum up, in a very short space of time, the internet has opened up many new opportunities to those people researching their Irish roots.

THE MAJOR ADMINISTRATIVE DIVISIONS

COUNTY

This division reflects the imposition of the English system
of local government in Ireland. Begun in the 12th century, the
32-county framework was completed with the creation of Wicklow in
1606. Their boundaries usually reflected the lordships of major
Gaelic families. For example, encompassing the 32 counties are
the four provinces of Ireland--Ulster, Connaught, Munster and
Leinster--which owe their origin to the pre-eminence of the
families O'Neill (Ulster), O'Brien (Munster), O'Connor (Connaught)
and MacMurrough (Leinster). It was these families who strived for
the High Kingship of all Ireland in the centuries before the
Norman invasion of the 12th century. The Irish families reflected
in the county divisions owed allegiance to these provincial kings.

BARONY

This is now an obsolete division, but in the 19th century it
was widely used. There were 327 baronies, which likewise tended
to reflect the holdings of Irish clans. Baronies and counties
became established in the government land surveys of the 17th
century.

POOR LAW UNION

Under the Poor Relief Act of 1838, Ireland was divided into
districts or "unions" in which the local rateable inhabitants were
to be financially responsible for the care of all paupers in their
areas. These unions, which didn't respect county boundaries, were
usually centered on a large market town. By 1850, 163 unions had
been created. The Local Government (Ireland) Act of 1898 adopted
the poor law union as the basic administrative division in place
of the civil parish and barony. The poor law unions of Ireland
were subdivided into 829 Registration Districts and 3,751 District
Electoral Divisions. Townlands were now arranged according to
these divisions, with parishes and baronies being retained only
as a means to make comparisons with records gathered before 1898.

PARISH

From the 17th century, the so-called civil parish, based on
the early christian and medieval monastic and church settlements,
was used extensively in various surveys. By the mid-19th century
the pattern of civil parishes was well established.

By 1841, the population of Ireland had risen to 8,175,124 and
this was reflected in changing parish boundaries. New parishes
were created by either subdividing larger ones or by withdrawing
townlands from adjoining parishes.

The civil parish essentially covered the same area as the
Established Church of Ireland parish, while the Roman Catholic
church, owing to the Reformation of the 16th century, had to adapt
itself to a new structure centered on towns and villages. There
are 2,428 civil parishes, which frequently break both barony and
county boundaries, indicating that they were drawn up at an
earlier period.

THE BARONIES OF COUNTY CORK

1. Bantry
2. Barretts
3. Barrymore
4. Bear
5. Carbery East (East Division)
6. Carbery East (West Division)
7. Carbery West (East Division)
8. Carbery West (West Division)
9. Condons & Clangibbon
10. Cork
11. Courceys
12. Duhallow
13. Fermoy
14. Ibane & Barryroe
15. Imokilly
16. Kerrycurrihy
17. Kinalea
18. Kinalmeaky
19. Kinnatalloon
20. Kinsale
21. Muskerry East
22. Muskerry West
23. Orrery & Kilmore

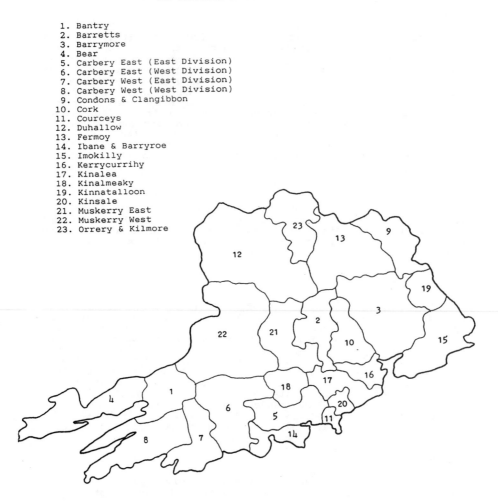

THE POOR LAW UNIONS OF THE PROVINCE OF CONNAUGHT

1. Althone
2. Ballina
3. Ballinasloe
4. Ballinrobe
5. Ballyshannon
6. Bawnboy
7. Belmullet
8. Boyle
9. Carrick on Shannon
10. Castlebar
11. Castlerea
12. Claremorris
13. Clifden
14. Dromore West
15. Galway
16. Glenamaddy

17. Gort
18. Killala
19. Loughrea
20. Manorhamilton
21. Mohill
22. Mount Bellew
23. Newport
24. Oughterard
25. Portumna
26. Roscommon
27. Sligo
28. Strokestown
29. Swineford
30. Tobercurry
31. Tuam
32. Westport

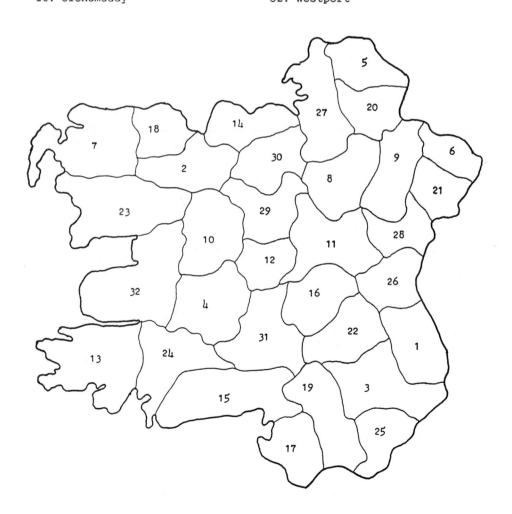

THE TOWNLANDS OF BAILIEBOROUGH PARISH, COUNTY CAVAN

1. Beckscourt
2. Bracklin
3. Cloverhill
4. Corglass
5. Corkish
6. Corlurgan
7. Cornanaff
8. Corraghy
9. Crocknahattin
10. Derrynure
11. Dromore
12. Drumacarrow
13. Drumanespick
14. Drumbannan
15. Drumkeery
16. Drumlon
17. Drumoosclin
18. Dundragon
19. Duneena

20. Galbolie
21. Gartnaneane
22. Greagharue
23. Greaghnamale
24. Killan
25. Lear
26. Leiter
27. Lisanalsk
28. Lisball
29. Lisgar
30. Lisnalea
31. Lurganbane
32. Monaghanoose
33. Pottle Lower
34. Pottle Upper
35. Rakeevan
36. Tanderagee
37. Urcher

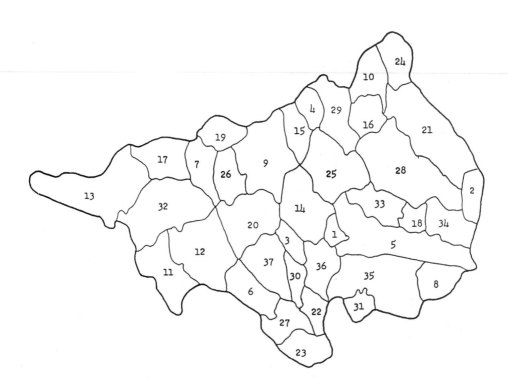

DIOCESE

Three ecclesiastical synods--Cashel in 1101, Rathbreasail in 1111 and Kells in 1152--imposed a diocesan organization of four provinces--Armagh, Cashel, Dublin and Tuam--each headed by an archbishop and, under them, 22 bishops in charge of as many dioceses. These diocesan boundaries have remained virtually constant to the present day and are in use by both the Catholic and Anglican churches. The number of dioceses has, however, varied with consolidation through time by both the Catholic and Anglican churches. Dioceses have little or no relation to the boundaries of the counties, the latter having been created long after the dioceses. In 1834, the Established Church of Ireland reduced the number of its provinces to two, namely Armagh and Dublin.

PROBATE DISTRICT

In 1858, a principal registry and eleven district registries were established for the purpose of proving wills and granting letters of administration. The boundaries of these probate districts followed either the county or barony divides.

TOWNLAND

The townland is the smallest and most ancient of Irish land divisions and is the goal of all family researchers in identifying the origin of their ancestors. The townland was named at an early period and usually referred to a very identifiable landmark in the local area such as a mountain, bog, oak forest, village, fort or church. The townland became standardized as a basic division in the 17th century surveys by people with little knowledge of the Irish language. As a consequence, many place names were either lost or had their meanings or construction altered.

A record of townland names, shapes, and sizes for all Ireland exist in the maps of the Ordnance Survey, completed in 1846, at the scale of six inches to one mile. Furthermore, *The General Alphabetical Index to the Townlands and Towns, Parishes and Baronies of Ireland*, better known as the "Townland Index," will identify all of Ireland's 60,462 townlands against their Ordnance Survey sheet number, county, barony, civil parish and poor law union.

A New Genealogical Atlas of Ireland, by the author (Genealogical Publishing Co., Baltimore, 1986), maps for every county of Ireland, her constituent civil parishes, baronies, dioceses, poor law unions and probate districts.

THE MAJOR RECORD OFFICES

General Register Office
Joyce House
8-11 Lombard Street East
Dublin 2
Telephone: 003531 6354000
Website: www.groireland.ie

Opening Hours: Monday to Friday 9.30am-12.30pm and 2.15pm-4.30pm

Fees:

5 year search of indexes for a given entry: £1.50
General search of indexes: £12.00
Photocopy of one entry from a register: £3.00 (or £1.50 when reference information supplied)
Short birth certificate: £3.50
Full birth, marriage and death certificate: £5.50

Remarks:

The General Register Office is currently engaged in the transfer of paper-based records to an electronic imaging system. In the Republic of Ireland local registrar offices still retain their respective original birth, marriage and death registers which are indexed (however not all local registrar offices facilitate searches of their registers).

Sources:

Civil registers of non-Catholic marriages 1845-1863; civil births, deaths and marriages for all Ireland 1864-1921; and for the Republic of Ireland from 1922.

General Register Office
Oxford House
49-55 Chichester Street
Belfast
BT1 4HL
Telephone: 028 90252022
Website: www.nisra.gov.uk/gro

Opening Hours: Monday to Friday 9.30am-4.00pm

Fees:

5 year search of index: £3.00
General search of indexes: £6.00 (this fee includes 4 verifications with option of further verifications at £1.00 each)
Short birth certificate: £7.00
Full birth, marriage and death certificate: £7.00
Priority certificate (within one hour of application): £10 extra
Assisted search of actual registers: £15 per hour (must be booked in advance)

Remarks:

Pre-1922 civil marriage records for Northern Ireland are held at local government level in the registrar offices maintained by each of the 26 local district councils. The General Register Office in Dublin holds copies of births, marriages and deaths registered in the whole of Ireland (which includes present-day Northern Ireland) up to December 1921.

Sources:

Civil registers of births and deaths for Northern Ireland from 1864 and civil marriages for Northern Ireland from 1922. This office holds indexes to births from 1864 and indexes to deaths and marriages from 1922.

National Archives
Bishop Street
Dublin 8
Telephone: 003531 4072300
Fax: 003531 4072333
Website: www.nationalarchives.ie

Opening Hours: Monday to Friday 10.00am-5.00pm

Fees:

None except for any photocopies of documents required. Photocopies can be made of most loose documents, but not of bound volumes or large fragile documents.

Remarks:

Apply for reader's ticket by filling form at front desk. Staff can answer queries but will not undertake research. Documents produced to readers from 10.00am-12.45pm and from 2.00pm-4.30pm.

Sources:

This office's record collection is very extensive and of all-Ireland significance. It holds diocesan, prerogative and civil wills; various 19th century census returns; 1901 and 1911 censuses; tithe books; Griffith's Valuation; convict transportation records; Estate records and microfilm copies of various Church of Ireland parish registers.

Public Record Office of Northern Ireland
66 Balmoral Avenue
Belfast
BT9 6NY
Telephone: 028 90255800
Fax: 028 90255999
Website: http://proni.nics.gov.uk

Opening Hours: Monday, Tuesday, Wednesday and Friday 9.15am-4.45 pm
               Thursday 9.15am-8.45pm

Fees:

No charge except for documents you require photocopied.

Remarks:

In the foyer fill in an application form for a reader's ticket. Staff willing to answer queries but will not undertake research. Microfilm copies of church registers are available on a self-service basis. Last orders for documents are 30 minutes before closing time.

Sources:

PRONI holds approximately 53 kilometres of records relating mainly to the nine counties of the province of Ulster (ie Counties Antrim, Armagh, Cavan, Donegal, Down, Fermanagh, Londonderry, Monaghan and Tyrone) . Records held include indexes to wills prior to 1858; wills from 1858 to 1900; trade and street directories; Griffith's Valuation; tithe books; 1901 census; estate papers; and microfilm copies of church registers of all denominations.

National Library of Ireland
Kildare Street
Dublin 2
Telephone: 003531 6030200
Fax: 003531 6766690
Website: www.nli.ie

Opening Hours: Monday to Wednesday 10.00am-9.00pm
            Thursday to Friday 10.00am-5.00pm
            Saturday 10.00am-1.00pm

Remarks:

The National Library requires users to apply for a reader's ticket although visitors can use the Library's genealogical service by simply signing the visitors' book. The Genealogical Service Room is manned by professional genealogists offering a free advice service to all personal callers to the Library. The Genealogical Service Room also holds a number of standard finding aids and reference material. This genealogical service is provided Monday to Friday 10.00am-4.45pm and Saturday 10.00am-12.30pm.

Manuscript reading room closes 30 minutes before main reading room. Manuscripts are not issued 12.30pm-2.00pm Monday to Friday; 5.00pm-6.00pm Monday to Wednesday; or after 7.00pm Monday to Wednesday.

Sources:

The National Library holds most pre-1880 Roman Catholic parish registers on microfilm (access to those for dioceses of Cashel, Kerry and Limerick require written permission from the relevant Bishop); Griffith's Valuation on microfiche; tithe books and 1766 Religious Census on microfilm. In addition the library holds a comprehensive collection of directories, photographs, newspapers, maps, manuscripts and estate papers.

Genealogical Office
2 Kildare Street
Dublin 2
Telephone: 003531 6030311/6030322
Fax: 003531 6621062
Website: www.nli.ie and select Office of The Chief Herald

Opening Hours: Monday to Friday 10.00am -12.30pm and 2.30pm-4.30pm

Remarks:

The Genealogical Office's principal function is heraldic. Applications to read manuscripts are made through the National Library of Ireland. There is no fee for consulting them but you will need a National Library reader's ticket.

Sources:

As the state heraldic authority the Genealogical Office holds manuscripts of the pedigrees of many families in both Gaelic and English. The office holds other important manuscript collections, including pedigree charts drawn up by Sir William Betham from all prerogative wills proved between 1536 and 1800. This is a significant record as the wills themselves no longer survive.

Royal Irish Academy
19 Dawson Street
Dublin 2
Telephone: 003531 6762570
Fax: 003531 6762346
Website: www.ria.ie

Opening Hours: Monday to Friday 10.30am-5.00pm

Remarks:

This learned society was founded in 1785 as a society for "promoting the study of science, polite literature and antiquities". Membership of the Academy, which currently stands at 275 members, is by election on the grounds of academic distinction.

Sources:

The Academy's library holds an extensive collection of ancient genealogical manuscripts, together with 17th century government records.

Linen Hall Library
17 Donegall Square North
Belfast
BT1 5GD
Telephone: 028 90321707
Website: www.linenhall.com

Opening Hours: Monday to Friday 9.30am-5.30pm
Saturday 9.30am-4.00pm

Remarks:

The Linen Hall is a public reference library

Sources:

This library has a large collection of books of genealogical interest, together with many early Belfast newspapers and a complete set of the Flax Growers' lists compiled in 1796.

Valuation Office Ireland
Irish Life Centre
Abbey Street Lower
Dublin 1
Telephone: 003531 8171000
Fax: 003531 8171180
Website: www.valoff.ie

Opening Hours: Monday to Friday 9.30am-12.30pm and 2.30pm-4.30pm

Fees:

A3 size photocopy of a section of a Griffith's Valuation map: £10
Photocopy of entire Griffith's Valuation map: £20

Sources:

This office holds a list of occupiers of property for the 26 counties of the Republic of Ireland. This list is broken into townlands within Rural Districts and into Rural Districts within Counties. The records go back to 1846. The same records for Northern Ireland are held in the Public Record Office of Northern Ireland. Of great significance to genealogists is the fact that the Griffith's Primary Valuation maps can be viewed here electronically as scanned images.

Registry of Deeds
King's Inn
Henrietta Street
Dublin
Telephone: 003531 6707500
Fax: 003531 8048408
Website: www.irlgov.ie/landreg

Opening Hours: Monday to Friday 10.00am-4.30pm

Fees:

Search per surname for 10 years: £2
General search: £10 per day
Certified copy of a "memorial": £4

Sources:

The Registry holds copies or "memorials" of deeds registered since 1708 together with their associated name and land indexes.

The Land Registers of Northern Ireland
Lincoln Building
27-45 Great Victoria Street
Belfast
BT2 7SL
Telephone: 028 90251555
Website: www.doeni.gov.uk/land

Opening Hours: Monday to Friday 10.00am-4.00pm

Sources:

This office administers the Registry of Deeds and Land Registry which have been public registries since 1708 and 1892 respectively.

Representative Church Body Library
Braemor park
Churchtown
Dublin 14
Telephone: 003531 4923979
Fax: 003531 4924770
Website: www.ireland.anglican.org/library/library.html

Opening Hours: Monday to Friday 9.30am-1.00pm and 1.45pm-5.00pm

Remarks:

The completion of an application form signed by an approved referee, and the payment of the subscription (£2 per annum or £30 for life) entitles members to borrow books. In 1994 the RCB began a new programme to publish old Church of Ireland parish registers.

Sources:

The RCB library is the Church of Ireland's principal repository for its archives and manuscripts which totals some 40,000 volumes. Sources include the original registers of some 600 Church of Ireland parishes and vestry books; 1740 Protestant Householders Lists; 1766 Religious Census; and 17th century hearth money rolls.

Presbyterian Historical Society of Ireland
Church House
Fisherwick Place
Belfast
BT1 6DW
Telephone: 028 90322284

Opening Hours: Monday, Tuesday, Thursday and Friday 10.00am-12.30pm
Wednesday: 10.00-12.30 and 1.30pm-3.30pm

Sources:

This society hold many Presbyterian registers, together with other material relating to Presbyterian families.

Society of Friends
Swanbrook House
Bloomfield Avenue
Donnybrook
Dublin 4
Telephone: 003531 6687157

Opening Hours: Thursday 11.00am-1.00pm

Sources:

In numerical terms the Quakers were insignificant in Ireland but they played an important role in industrial development. The records of births, marriages, deaths and wills kept by Quakers date back to the 17th century.

LDS Family History Centres
Website: www.familysearch.org

The website of the Church of Jesus Christ of Latter-Day Saints (Mormons) identifies 5 Family History Centres in Ireland:

Cork Ireland
Scarsfield Road
Wilton
Cork

Dublin Ireland
The Willows
Finglas Road
Glasnevin
Dublin 11

Limerick Ireland
Doradoyle Road
Limerick

Belfast Northern Ireland
403 Holywood Road
Belfast

Londonderry Northern Ireland
Racecourse Road
Belmont Estate
Londonderry

Remarks:

Owing to limited staff the Family History Centres in Ireland have limited opening hours and mail inquiries are not responded to. These centres are primarily for the use of local residents. Visitors from overseas should check the holdings of the LDS Centre in their home country before travelling to Ireland.

Sources:

Family History Centres hold microfilm copies of the indexes to civil birth, marriage and death registers up to 1958; civil birth registers 1864-1881 and 1900-1913; civil marriages 1845-1870; and civil deaths 1864-1870. They also hold the International Genealogical Index.

THE HERITAGE CENTRES OF IRELAND

The Irish Genealogical Project (IGP) became a reality in 1990. The IGP envisaged the establishment of a network of centres, usually on a county basis, to computerise the major record sources and to service family history queries within their catchment areas. The following sources were identified as the major sources to be computerised:

- Pre-1922 civil birth, marriage and death registers
- Pre-1900 Church baptismal, marriage and burial registers of all denominations
- Gravestone Inscriptions
- 1901 census
- Mid-19th century Griffith's Valuation
- Early-19th century Tithe Applotment Books

Ireland's network of genealogy centres have built up databases for their local areas that can't be matched by any other organisation. If you lack the time, interest and/or access to record sources to pursue your family history it makes very good sense to commission a genealogy centre to search their database and compile a report into your family history.

As genealogy centres don't receive public funding to operate a research service it means they are obliged to charge commercial rates for genealogical research. It must be stressed that genealogy centres are not libraries, if you wish to conduct your own research through record sources then you should approach the relevant record offices (see Glossary of The Major Record Offices).

I think it is fair to say that if you have already exhausted the major sources of genealogical research in Ireland, ie church registers, civil registers, census returns and census substitutes, there is probably little additional information to be gained from commissioning a genealogy centre to search their database.

I believe there is one circumstance in which genealogy centres offer real value for money. If all you know about your ancestor is their county of origin then the database of the appropriate genealogy centre is probably the only realistic hope of confirming your ancestral origins. Without the help of such a database you hold insufficient information to make basic decisions about which sources to search. In the age before databases a fairly precise knowledge (usually a townland or parish address) of where an ancestor came from was the key to unlocking family history.

IRISH GENEALOGY CENTRES

COUNTY	CENTRE	CONTACT	ADDRESS	PHONE
Antrim	Ulster Historical Foundation	Shane Mc Ateer	12 College Square East, Belfast, BT1 6DD	028 90332288
Armagh	Armagh Ancestry	Grace Greer	St Patricks Trian, 38A Upper English Sreet, Armagh, BT61 7BA	028 37521802
Carlow	Carlow Genealogy Project	Mary Moore	Old School ,College Street, Carlow	00353 50330850
Cavan	Cavan Genealogy Research Centre	Mary Sullivan	Cana House, Farnham Street, Cavan	00353 494361094
Clare	Clare Heritage & Genealogical Centre	Antoinette O Brien	Church Street, Corofin, Co Clare	00353 65683795 5
Cork (City)	Cork City Ancestral Project	Karen O Riodan	C/O County Library, Farranlea Road, Cork City	00353 21434643 5
Cork (North & East)	Mallow Heritage Centre		27/28 Bank Place, Mallow, County Cork	00353 2250302
Cork (West)	West Cork Heritage Centre		Bandon, Co Cork	
Derry	Genealogy Centre	Brian Mitchell	Heritage Library, 14 Bishop Street, Derry BT48 6PW	028 71269792
Donegal	Donegal Ancestry	Joan Patton	Old Meeting House, Ramelton, Co Donegal	00353 7451266
Down	Ulster Historical Foundation	Shane McAteer	12 College Square East, Belfast, BT1 6DD	028 90332288
Dublin (City)	Dublin Heritage Group		C/O Ballyfermot Library, Ballyfermot, Dublin 10	00353 16269324
Dublin (North)	Fingal Heritage Group	Bernadette Marks	Carnegie Library, North Street, Swords, Co Dublin	00353 18400080
Dublin (South)	Dun Laoghaire Heritage Society	Mairead Walsh	Moran Park House, Dun Laoghaire, Co Dublin	00353 12806961
Fermanagh	Heritage World	Eoin Kerr	Heritage Centre, Pomeroy Road, Donaghmore BT70 3HG, Co Tyrone	028 87761306
Galway (East)	East Galway Family History Society	Cora Fitzgerald	Woodford Heritage Centre, Woodford, Co Galway	00353 50949309
Galway (West)	West Galway Family History Society	Marie Mannion	Unit 3, Venture Centre, Liosbaun Estate, Tuam Road, Galway	00353 91756737
Kerry	Killarney Genealogical Centre	Marie O Sullivan	Cathedral Walk, Killarney, Co Kerry	
Kildare	Kildare Heritage Centre	Karel Kiely	C/O Kildare Co Library, Newbridge, Co Kildare	00353 45433602
Kilkenny	Kilkenny Archaeological Society	Mary Flood	Rothe House, Parliament Street, Co Kilkenny	00353 5622893
Laois	Laois/Offaly Family History Centre	John Kearney	Bury Quay, Tullamore, Co Offaly	00353 50621421
Leitrim	Leitrim Genealogy Centre		C/O Co Library, Ballinamore, Co Leitrim	00353 7844012
Limerick	Limerick Ancestry		The Granary, Michael Street, Limerick	00353 61410777

IRISH GENEALOGY CENTRES

COUNTY	CENTRE	CONTACT	ADDRESS	PHONE
Longford	Longford Heritage Centre	Mary Boland	1 Church Street, Battery Road, Longford	00353 4341235
Louth	Louth County Library		Roden Place, Dundalk, Co Louth	00353 429353190
Mayo (North)	Mayo North Family Heritage Centre	Fiona Forde	Enniscoe, Castlehill, Ballina, Co Mayo	00353 9631809
Mayo (South)	South Mayo Family Research Centre	Gerard M Delaney	Main Street, Ballinrobe, Co Mayo	00353 9241214
Meath	Meath Heritage & Genealogy Centre	Noel French	Town Hall, Castle Street, Trim, Co Meath	00353 4636633
Monaghan	Monaghan Ancestry	Theo Mc Mahon	6 Tully, Monaghan, Co Monaghan	00353 50621421
Offaly	Laois/Offaly Family History Centre	John Kearney	Bury Quay, Tullamore, Co Offaly	
Roscommon	Co Roscommon Genealogy Centre	Mary Skelly	Church Street, Strokestown, Co Roscommon	00353 7833380
Sligo	Co Sligo Heritage & Genealogy Society	John O Hara	Aras Redden, Temple Street, Sligo	00353 7143728
Tipperary (Cashel & Emly)	Tipperary Heritage Unit	Anne Moloney	The Bridewell, St Michael Street, Tipperary	00353 6252725
Tipperary (North)	Tipperary North Family Research Centre	Nora O Meara	The Gatehouse, Kickham Street, Nenagh, Co Tipperary	00353 6733850
Tipperary (South)	Bru Boru Heritage Centre	Deirdre Walsh	Rock of Cashel, Cashel, Co Tipperary	00353 6261122
Tyrone	Heritage World	Eoin Kerr	Heritage Centre, Pomeroy Road, Donaghamore BT70 3HG, Co Tyrone	028 87761306
Waterford	Waterford Heritage Centre	Carmel Meehan	Jenkins Lane, St Patricks Church, Waterford	00353 51876123
Westmeath	Dun Na Si Heritage Centre	Caroline Ganley	Knockdomney, Moate, Co Westmeath	00353 90281183
Wexford	Wexford Genealogy Centre	Patrick Stafford	Yola Farmstead, Tagoat, Co Wexford	00353 5332611
Wicklow	County Wicklow Family History Centre	Joan Kavanagh	Wicklow's Historic Gaol, Kilmantin Hill, Wicklow	00353 40420126

For more details about Genealogy Centres visit www.irishroots.net on the internet.